Best Student

Creative Non-Fiction

Best Student Creative Non-Fiction
Champlain College Anthology Series

Jamie Anmac

Nina Boutsikaris

Taylor Covington

Erin Gleeson

Amanda Northrop

Jessica DiNapoli

Patience Hurlburt-Lawton

John R. Gunther

Jaime Berry

Ashley DeFelice

Christina Etre

Marissa Caan

Alexa Ercolano

Christian Belekewicz

Emily Murnane

Pat Willwerth

Agata Ayrapetova

Editor: Larry Connolly

 Champlain Books
A division of Barnes | MacQueen Publishing Resources

Champlain Books
a division of Barnes | MacQueen Publishing Resources
47 Maple St., Suite 206
Burlington, Vermont 05401
www.ChamplainBooks.com
www.barnesmacqueen.com
Printed in the United States of America
First Edition: June 2014
ISBN: 978-0-9884523-7-4

Cover and interior design by Matthew Kedzierski

Acknowledgments
The Champlain College Publishing Initiative (CCPI) was created in order to provide Champlain College students with first-hand experience in the field of publishing. CCPI's mission is to play an active part in the great experiment that is publishing in the twenty-first century.

To everyone brave enough to tell the truth

Table of Contents

About the Anthology

These stories were written by people very much like you.

Most anthologies feature the work of experienced, professional writers, and it's easy to assume that there is an unbridgeable gap between them and the apprentice writer. They are older and more widely traveled, they have more time to devote to their writing, they have friends in important magazines and publishing companies, they have expense budgets—you could come up with a hundred reasons why you can't do what they have done. Some of those reasons may even be valid.

In Best Student Creative Non-Fiction, though, you'll find a collection of pieces written by students taking writing courses at college. None was writing full time, or writing professionally (though some have gone on to do so), yet all these pieces are interesting, rich, readable, full of surprises—exactly what you want from a piece of writing. They also show that you can take risks with your writing, and when you take risks the results, often to your own surprise, may be even more interesting and more readable.

Please don't be intimidated by what you read. No student writes like this at the beginning of a semester, or in a first draft. Every one of these pieces has been through more than one draft, and in the case of the longer pieces, probably half a dozen drafts. In some cases the piece started out as something completely different. Each section begins with a shorter piece, one that may even have been the product of an in-class exercise, and then moves into more developed pieces that graft the skills into a more developed and ambitious piece.

What will come across, I hope, is that writing is not as complicated as it may seem, and it certainly doesn't take years of professional experience or an M.F.A. Mostly it takes being courageous, being alert, asking questions, taking detailed notes, thinking long and hard about your subject, and then sitting down and talking to the reader, person to person. Then revising. You can do all that.

About Creative Non-Fiction

Creative non-fiction is a form of writing that explores both the world around you, and the world inside you. It is non-fiction that goes beyond simply providing information: it asks what that information means to the writer, and how to turn the subject into a compelling experience for a reader. It uses the writing tactics of the novelist and even the poet, and tackles questions usually asked by the journalist and the essayist.

The impulse of the writer of creative non-fiction is curiosity, and the best writers are curious to explore both the universe around them and the universe within, and to look for connections and clashes between those two fields.

In theory, this is pretty straightforward—after all, we are affected internally by things happening around us, and the changes inside us affect the way we see the physical world and act in it.

Writing about this duality, though, requires a particular set of skills—not so much of writing in the technical sense as skills of observation (both outside and in), of understanding. If what we write about our inner quests is interesting but we are incurious about the outside world, then half of what we write is mere painted background scenery, flat and flimsy. If we're eager to investigate the world around us but ignore its effects on the self, everything we write sounds oddly cold, or hollow. To combine the two requires a culmination of all the skills we've been considering so far in this collection, and maybe even some others.

Finally, there's the issue of blending. How do you combine introspection with storytelling and perhaps also the skills of a journalist or researcher?

And how do you do so in a way that is tailored to your particular subject, your own particular investigative journey, so it doesn't read like every other memoir or extended essay?

Creative non-fiction has its own discipline. It demands that you be honest, but allows you to be imaginative. It offers you easy structures, but then insists you do something different. You need to reject the temptation to be self-indulgent and soft, but equally you need to reject the temptation to hide behind hard facts and figures. If you find the balance, though, creative non-fiction allows you to speak in your own voice and speak from every dimension of your being.

You will work to discover what you most deeply want to write about, and how to turn those ideas, memories, concerns, insights and passions into a series of pieces of writing that are intelligent, moving, and unforgettable.

Tim Brookes
Champlain College, Burlington, Vermont
January 2014

[one]

Voices

Brain

Jamie Anmac

"Ekrem," I tell my Turkish fiancé, "I am hungry. Do you want to go get dinner now?"

"Sure. What would you like to eat?"

"I don't know. Maybe… soup."

"OK. Have you ever had brain soup?"

"Brain soup? Uh, no, I can't say that I have. Why?"

"Because tonight you will try brain soup. Would you like to try?"

"Uh…sure. I guess so. I'll try anything at least once."

"Good! Ten minutes we will go."

We walk a block down the street to a small hole-in-the-wall restaurant. We seat ourselves and a waiter quickly comes over and takes our order. Now we are waiting for the soup to arrive.

"So Ekrem, what animal brain do they use to make the soup?"

"Animal? Who says they use animal?"

"Well, what other species would they use to make brain soup with?"

"It is human," he says with a smirk.

"Now I know you're joking."

"You think so? You will see."

The waiter arrives and sets the soup on the table.

"Well, what do you think?"

"Hang on, Ekrem. I haven't tried it yet. Do you squirt the lemon in the soup?"

"Yes. And you can put garlic and vinegar in it. Would you like some?"

"Sure, I guess."

He dumps a spoonful of garlic and vinegar into the soup, and squirts half a lemon in as well. I start to eat.

"How is it?"

"Well… it is kind of what I expected." The brain is gray with lines running through and even though it is chopped up it still looks like a brain. The soup itself is creamy but doesn't have a distinct flavor except for the vinegar, lemon, and garlic. And the texture of the brain kind of reminds me of eating mushrooms.

"So, you like it?"

"Well… I am not crazy about it. It is okay to eat once, but I don't think I would eat it again because just the thought of me eating brain is kind of grossing me out."

"Grossing you out? What does it mean?"

"Grossing me out? Uh… it means disgusting."

"Oh, OK."

We eat in silence for a minute. Then I start coughing.

"Why are you coughing? You don't like? Would you like something else?"

"No, it is not from the soup. Remember, I told you yesterday. I think I am getting sick."

"Don't say 'sick.'"

"Why?"

"Because in my language 'sick' means 'penis' or 'to fuck.' So don't say sick. Say you are ill."

"Do you spell 'sick' the same way as in English?"

"No, we spell it S-I-K. But it sounds the same."

"Good to know." I take a spoonful of soup and stop. "So wait… is that why your parents looked at me funny yesterday when I was coughing and they asked what was wrong with me and I said I am sick?"

"Yes."

"Are there any other words I should beware of?"

"Uh… I am not sure. I will let you know when you say them."

The Last Night As This

Nina Boutsikaris

"Where'd Dad go?" I ask. It's a question that will come up again numerous times that year, for different reasons. She nods toward the parking lot, keeping her arms crossed on her chest, as if she is holding close some burden I know nothing of, and I suppose I don't.

"Getting the car," she says, gesturing with her head.

I swear, I have never seen a moon like this, so incredibly bright, casting a path on the river that makes forever seem not that long at all. Everything is breathing sweet and low with the late spring breeze. I follow my mother down the hill to the end of the pier, past the Clairmont Apartments, which are eerily empty due to an architectural flaw that left them partly uninhabitable. I lean against the wooden railing and watch my mother watch the sky.

"Amazing," she says. "This is why life is so... just...."

I think I know what she means. Sometimes it seems that life is merely moments. A moon can fill up so many. The water laps at the dock, licking the pilings that have begun to look lazy as they dip into the river with seeming nonchalance. From somewhere through the night drift the few notes of a saxophone's lonesome ballad.

"Quite an evening."

Startled, I jerk my head to look behind me. A leathery man in cowboy boots and a half-buttoned plaid shirt shifts his backpack. Like dried up riverbeds, the lines on his face are drawn together underneath his eyes, which sparkle even in this hazy light. My mother watches him. She smiles.

"Yes, it is."

"Last time I was here there was a girl in a red dress. Black hair... skinny as a 'lectric wire."

I can tell he sees her when he closes his eyes and jams his thumbs into his front jean pockets.

"There was a moon just like this one. Strange really, almost too big, like some balloon ready to burst." He throws his head back, mouth open and slack. "It was her birthday. She just wanted to dance. So I danced with her, right here on this pier."

He lifts his arm slightly in front of him, slipping it around an imaginary waist.

"She was alone in the world, or so she said, and for those few minutes I was the only one."

Is he humming? Maybe it's me.

"I been all 'round this world. It's a beautiful world."

I feel my mother being silent, letting the man speak where perhaps she would have spoken. She hardly even breathes, and I follow her lead. I am enchanted—by this moon, this man, this night. The last night before my mother left my father.

"Yes… I've been all around this world. But it's funny how I end up here, with this same moon. 'Course, it's the same moon everywhere."

He waits. We say nothing.

"She said, 'Love is the highest law.'" He is almost whispering now. "'For if we do not embrace each other, what hope do we have in this life?' Yep. Something like that."

I expect that was exactly what she said.

Suddenly I am wondering how many people have heard this story, how many people he has poured this weight onto. Perhaps we are the first, perhaps the hundredth. The mystery of it leaves me thirsty. I lick my lips and taste salt. Then my father honks the horn from the street. It burns my ears and leaves me oddly annoyed. I am not ready.

"Well." My mother is smoothing her collar now. "Have a lovely evening."

The man tips his hat and as we walk away I sense my mother's eyes widen. A tiny smile spreads across her face, twitching from the corners of her pursed lips. There is something new between us, something fresh, at least for now. A secret.

"You know," she says, without looking at me, "he probably never saw that girl again."

I nod. I'm certain.

[two]

Setting

Old Hippie God

Taylor Covington

At the end of a dusty road, beyond gray and faded-green trees, past
a chipped and peeling orange Cadillac of a run-away bride, there is
the Story House. This is not the real name of the dwelling dozing
heavily off the highway in the warm hills of Austin, Texas. Its real
name is something earthy and brown, at one with nature, but there
it sits, the incarnation of a long-dead hippie, his idyllic escape still
filled with Texan people. It rims the dip of a hill, the grass tumbling
down from ivy that stalks up the back of the house, all the way down
into a creek, where the grass lunged forward into wide reeds and
a tree with a rope-swing. We slept there on that hill. In tents, on
sleeping bags, on the old ground itself, just like our ancestors. And
we listened. We listened to the crickets, to the worried question of
the owl, to the crunch of leaves by wind. There, gazing up at bejew-
eled stars on the throat of the Sky Goddess, we listened to the creak
of summer.

The house itself is old. The wood groans but never breaks under
the continuous tap of rough feet. Doors swing open and shut unhur-
ried and the walls, decorated by a smearing of dedication and good
will, keep out the coyote spirits. Every room is different, themed by
cowboys, or the ocean, or the voracious presence of animals. For a
moment, we are spinning among the rings of Saturn in the Space
Room, or listening to Ella Fitzgerald croon away the Commies in
the 50s Room. The Old Hippie God who owned the house collected
treasures of the past and trinkets of the future and placed them here,
a sentient being overlooking all time and space. He aimed for smiles.
He actively grasped at dreams and wants and desires and made them
reality just for a moment of quiet contentment. Inside his house
that surpassed the makings of a home, he put us to sleep under the
coverings of an unimaginable, promising future.

I call it the Story House because of the bottom level. It has no walls, only wooden pillars and staircases leading to rooms unknown. But it is the faces in the frames, on the pillars, on the staircases that make it so memorable. Just as in the rooms, the hippie god collected dolls, baubles, figurines, tiny stone faces of the sun and moon, lunchboxes, ceramic dog pins, cats made from lollipop wrappers, magnets of cowboys, tiny crossbows, flags, prayers on stones, colored mirrors, wooden mermaids and shiny toy guns. He strung up paper dolls from the ceiling, doilies on the fans, birds of gold and silver in the corners, and threw checkered plaid over the tables. The flagstones, baked warm during the day, were worshipped as they pictured rising suns, waters in the lakes near burning villages, an Aztec priest waking his jaguar son, a Virgin greeting the world—the gods were pleased.

These are faces—of memories new and old and still to come. In the summer, we clamored into the creek, yelling and running and singing. At night, we'd eat sweet blueberry pie and soft vanilla ice cream. We drank tea and wished for the moment to last a bit longer. But that's the covenant of the Old Hippie God: your story must end, but it will always be here, sleeping among the rest—in the old Story House.

Coosane

Erin Gleeson

The rain knows this house well. It knows the patched white-stucco exterior, it knows the cerulean blue border above the doorway, the one that matches the short wooden fence surrounding the front, behind the shrubbery, which is home to a ram's skull decorated into the hedge, home to little alice-blue and cotton-white flowers.

Yes, the rain knows this house. It has danced along its slate-shingled roof and pitter-pattered against the windows shielded by Irish lace, windows that are display cases to figurines: a ceramic Mother Mary, a staple in any county home. And the front walk—the rain has collected in the ruts, the dips and dents in a patch-worked pathway. It pools around the cornflower-blue ceramic tile, mosaicked within the gray-stone pieces. Other patches claim the color of rose, and my favorite few harbor nautical sketches of boats and waves. The rain knows this path, this eclectic collection of colors and tiles, a speckled and cracked foundation.

The rain has known this house for hundreds of years. It knows the gates, the fields, and the stream that field-straw boats have sailed in. It knows the stinging nettle, and the dock-leaf growing beside it. It knows the mountains guarding from behind, and the latching green gate keeping vigil from the road; it knows Rover, the dog shepherding the sheep and hearts of old men. The rain knows the old tractor in the field; it has left its signs of moss and rust, which have made home along its metal jacket and old wheels, roving through its aged body. The rain has been here before; it has left its liquid song.

I've been here before, too.

The drizzle may have found its way inside, during the days of thatched roofs or broken slate, but it is not as well acquainted with the interior as I. I'm not sure it has fallen against the stained-glass squares of the window in the white front door, which hides beneath its own shelter of stone and stucco. Nor has it painted itself over those worn goldenrod walls. I'm quite sure it has not taken hold of the warm knob, letting itself in.

The rain wants to know what dwells inside because it leaves anyone curious, to know only part of a whole so well. It begins to wonder about the other half, and so it clings to my clothes, my raincoat, my sea-blue scarf; it settles itself into the copper rings of my hair and holds tight to my eyelashes. I track puddles behind me, on the honey-brown linoleum floor. To my left, a small dining room, never used, and a flight of steep and narrow stairs, leading the way to bedrooms in which teams of children have lived, where my grandfather lived, where my father lived, and his beloved grandfather too. Straight ahead leads to the kitchen, tiled in gray-blue, burnt orange and cream, a kitchen too small, too crowded and cluttered to use. Bags of potatoes, an old oven, a portable stove-top, mops and brooms older than I—it is a kitchen that has not been used for a kitchen's purpose since matriarchy reigned. And a bathroom off to the side, with the yellowing mirror and petite porcelain toilet bowl, a white stream of gray-day light shining through the tiny window.

The rain does not take any of these routes. It follows the tingling warm scent, a true comfort-scent, of a freshly lit peat fire. We veer to the right, into the still-pumping heart of the house. Not much bigger than the rest of the rooms, this one is a living memory—the kind one cannot shake from the mind like rain from a coat. I remove my jacket, brushing rain from my hair, and sit in a throne of shabby scarlet and chipped wood.

This room is over three hundred years of mothers, fathers, children, and welcome strangers. The fading floor has worn the tracks of dirt and grass and manure. On the wall is a mirror and above that mirror on the wall is wedged a fading palm-leaf folded into the shape of a cross. Along the walls are clocks, calendars, an old lamp and a framed painting of Jesus, illuminated by a plastic red light bulb. A radio, older than me, sits on a metal chair. African relics are scattered around the room, figurines that have traveled with a priest brother. A large cerulean hutch sits in the corner, shelving boxes of Barry's tea, cups and glasses, jars of spices and spreads, tins of biscuits, cookies and breads, and bottles and bottles of spirits: whiskey, scotch and some "real old mountain dew"— Irish moonshine. Beside the hutch, next to the one window, is a folding table for sitting, eating and talking of Christian flaws, dwindling economies and mingled memories.

The fireplace demands the attention of the room. How does one paint a picture of such a fireplace? It has the face of the old men who stoke it. It is covered in a medley of moss-green, gray, cream and copper and brown, with patches of robin-egg blue. Arms hang from the hearth: one with hooks for pots, which get more use than anything in the kitchen; one from a poker and other tools; and one from which a bulky set of binoculars hang. On the floor sits the teakettle and pots. Against the wall stands a hand-carved blackthorn hiking cane with bumps and knobs, though it's smooth to the touch. And there, on the wooden boards, is Cat, who finds warmth and solace next to the growing fire. This one-eyed, aged, golden feline breaks the guard of old countrymen, these old bachelors, receiving scraps and affectionate clicks and clucks.

These countrymen are the voices and creaks in this house: My kindred-spirit teacher, the silent millionaire, the laughing deaf husband, and the timid host—brothers of my gentle-spoken and mischievous-eyed grandfather. They are bits and pieces of my father. They are bits and pieces of me. They are the old house, as I must be. I remain in my scarlet throne and listen to the rain outside, dancing on the slate roof and on the shadow-box windows, falling into puddles on nautical tiles. Falling towards patchwork fields and mountains and streams. Falling, outside, against trees and wooden ladders, fences and shrubs, rams and sheep and their bleating young. Falling on a house—Coosane—beyond three hundred years, tucked between a mountain and a latching, swinging green gate.

A Night On The Town

Amanda Northrop

I pulled into the Woody's Sports Bar lot, parking between a familiar Nissan and a Jeep. Through the window, I could see several of my mother's friends. Mark, my former little league coach was standing in the middle of the aisle, his huge Irish body taking up most of the space between the bar and booths. His left arm was flailing and his right hand was clasped around a huge stein of beer. He seemed to have everyone in stitches.

I stepped out of the car and took a deep breath. I had been at the bar earlier that day with my mother, watching the women's basketball game, and nobody seemed to mind that a sixteen-year-old was there. I wasn't so sure if it would still be okay, but I had promised to pick up Mrs. Meyers and drive her home.

Woody's was the only bar in Middletown, so I recognized nearly half of the patrons. My old neighbor, whose son had killed himself a year before, was at a small round table to my left, barely recognizable behind a baseball cap and screen of cigarette smoke. Vicodin Man was shooting pool in the back left corner of the bar. His awkward frame seemed stiffer than usual, and I made a mental note to find out if he had anything stronger than the normal stuff.

I turned right and strolled between the bar and booths. As I approached, Mark put his beer down and bellowed, "There's the beautiful girl!" He leaned close to my ear and I could feel the whiskers on his face and smell beer and chicken wings. "Do you want a drink, baby?"

I looked over at the bartender, Charlene, whose kids I used to babysit.

"Do you think Charlene will care? She knows I'm not twenty-one."

"Oh sure. I'll order the drink for myself, and then you can have it. Just hide it under the table. Ask her for a soda or something, so she'll think you're drinking Coke." He winked an enormous eye and stumbled over to the bar.

I turned to the booth and said hi to Mrs. Meyers. She was tanked, as usual, and I asked her when she wanted to go home.

"Honey," she slurred, "I don't ever want to go home." Her voice started to quiver and her face bunched up. "It's so fucking sad there, and Rich always needs me to do this and do that, and the kids won't help him out, so it's just me taking care of him and he could die soon because of that fucking cancer and I don't want to deal with any of it." She had started sobbing and her mascara was running down her face. "Honey, I'm sorry. I'll be happy now."

"Here ya go, kiddo." Mark had returned with what looked like a Coke. He saw Mrs. Meyers and put his arms around her. "Oh, baby, what's wrong?"

Mrs. Meyers began to shake, and at first I thought we were going to bring her home right then and there, but then I realized she was laughing. She gave Mark a rather intimate kiss and turned to me.

"Let's go out back. Mark has some great stuff," she whispered, though most of the bar probably heard.

"Yeah," Mark added, "bet you've never had anything like it." He stood up, hitting his head on the low-hanging light fixture. "Follow me."

I sucked down my rum and Coke and followed Mark and Mrs. Meyers out the back door of the bar, immediately recognizing where I was. A small concrete parking lot extended along the back of the building. Further beyond that was a small pond with a rock beach. I had come to that pond numerous times on my bicycle not that many years before, skipping rocks, fishing, and jumping the concrete ramp on my bike. Even in the dark, I could make out the rock where I had my first kiss.

"Hey. Kid. Try this." Mark's voice brought me back into the present. He handed me a joint and I took a long drag. The smoke tasted stale and harsh. I handed it to Mrs. Meyers.

"I've had better."

Mark didn't hear me. He was swinging Mrs. Meyers around, arms around her waist. He lost his footing and they both crashed hard to the ground. I ran over to save the joint from certain destruction. I was beginning to feel tipsy myself. I took another huge drag off the joint.

"Mrs. Meyers, don't you think you need to go home?" I exhaled a giant cloud into the night.

"No!" Her lip began shaking again. "I'm not going. Mark, take me home with you. I don't want to do this any more." She began to wail. "Oh God, my life is so awful and nobody cares. They all take and take and I can't give anymore."

I thought about Emily, her daughter, who I had always longed to be friends with, and Rich, who was probably at home worried that his wife was dead and that he'd have to go through the last months of his life alone.

"C'mon. Let's go. I need to drive you home, and I can't be out too late. My mom will worry."

"Fuck your mom." She was getting nasty.

"Mark, I'll be in the car. Can you get her there?"

"Sure," he replied. He turned to Mrs. Meyers and began rubbing her hair.

I walked the long way around the building so I could keep the joint going. My head felt heavy and my whole body was buzzing. As I rounded the corner to the front of the bar, I saw Vicodin Man getting into the Nissan next to my car.

"Hey," I shouted. He paused. "Wait."

I handed him the joint.

"Thanks, darling." His voice was thick and raspy at the same time.

"Do you have anything new?" I asked.

"Sure. Get in the car so Charlene don't see you through the window."

I sank into the sporty car. The floor and console were littered with empty Camel cigarette packs. Vicodin Man opened the center console and my heart jumped when I saw the bottles of pills. Finally, something worth it.

"Here. These are extra strength, so take a half at a time." He put six pills into my open palm. "That's twelve bucks."

"How 'bout ten and the rest of the joint?" He looked in my eyes and without looking away, grabbed the joint from my hand.

"Thanks." I pulled myself out of the car and opened my own door. As soon as I was in my car I popped three pills into my mouth and chewed them. The bitter taste almost made me gag. Half a pill at a time? What did he think I was, a pussy?

I saw Mark dragging Mrs. Meyers around the corner. As they approached, I could tell she was almost out. He opened the passenger door of my car and tried to place her dead weight into the seat gently. I started the car.

"Thanks, Mark."

"Sure." He bent down and peered into the car. "Hey, if you ever need anything, I got plenty. Just call me."

"Yeah, sure," I said, putting the car in reverse. He closed the door and waved. Next to me, Mrs. Meyers had slumped into the seat, her head lolling about as I pulled the car out of the driveway.

[three]

Characters

The Kitchen Table

Patience Hurlburt-Lawton

I swung open her front screen door. My eyes scanned the rustic kitchen, darting from the small television on the counter to Gramps, sitting at the table wearing a red T-shirt under his flannel jacket. He was eighty-two, with gray lines in dark hair and on his stubbled chin. White socks and black slippers covered his swollen ankles. His eyes shifted down to his large hands. I looked toward the thick, wooden bathroom door to my left. Mom stood in the corner, walking to me like her bones were aching. Her gray sweatshirt hung loose on her arms, extending out, reaching for me. "Baby," she whispered, her blue eyes magnified by moisture and redness. "I'm so sorry, Baby." I tucked my head between her shoulder and neck, the ends of her dirty-blonde hair brushing against my cheek. I melted from her arms down to the wooden chair at the kitchen table.

I was still wearing the black Nike shorts and dark blue tank top I had slept in. I had no shoes on. On the table in front of me were Gram's empty pack of Virginia Slims 120s and a can of Diet Pepsi with a straw in it. It was half full.

A large-print crossword puzzle book was open beside me on the table, in front of the chair she sat in at night, under the lamp that was now turned off. I spent my evenings sitting with her here, the woodstove radiating orange heat in the winter, or a cool breeze pushing through the open window in the summer. After taking a shower she sat down at the table with me, wearing her light-pink nightgown, her white hair, still wet, brushed back. She tapped her pen against the table while her green eyes danced along the page of another crossword. The kitchen was quiet, except for the voices trickling from the television and her occasional humming under the lamp's light. We laughed often, but shared these brief moments of silence both at her wooden kitchen table and in her white Ford

Focus—sitting so close our arms brushed, feeling the warmth from the other's skin.

Her jewelry was now in a pile on the table: her thin engagement ring with a diamond smaller than a pea and her gold wedding band; a thick class ring with a blue stone in the middle, the letters worn and smooth; a thin-band watch, and the necklace she wore everyday with three silver stars hanging from the chain. Her round, smudged glasses rested beside an orange bottle with Catherine C. Hurlburt written on the white label. Take 1 tab. by mouth twice a day. Five pills were left at the bottom. The remote for the garage was hidden under three Bic lighters, next to her inhaler. Everything had been touched by her hours ago. She could have been in the other room.

Thirsty Cab Driver

Jessica DiNapoli

It is dark. It is raining. There are three women on Cumberland Square, Dublin, walking up to three separate cars. I am the only woman approaching a cab. I am the only woman who is not a prostitute.

When I get closer to the cab I notice it is not running, unlike the other two cars, and the cab driver is stepping out of his vehicle. I walk faster towards him. "Excuse me!" The rain falls harder and I try to protect the thin toilet tissue that is wrapped around my bloody hand. "Wait! I-I'm sorry, but are you off duty?"

The cab driver clumsily spins around to face me. Technically he is plump but plump is associated with light-hearted chubbiness and, often, with the idea of someone being "pleasantly plump" and, sure, this man is pleasant but I do not know that yet and there is something heavy looking about his physique, his movements, even his reddened face. His stomach hangs low over his belt and he grunts as he hoists up his pants. He chews gum, pushes his big square glasses up the bridge of his nose (and let me say this about his most peculiar nose: It is small, dainty, and oddly perfect but does not at all fit on his meaty face), and looks me up and down before smiling. His cheeks are ridden with patches of whiskers and his froggish mouth is outlined with two long, thin lips that reveal stained but neatly aligned teeth.

"Eh, well, I've been off duty fer a bit, but…." He hesitates, coughs, and then without warning breaks into a song. "Yooooouuuuurrrrrr hairrrrr is lovelyyyyyyyyy my laaaaaaaadddyyyyyyyy so I will be sure to take you whereverrrrrrr yoooouuuuuu neeeeeeeddddd toooo gooooooooooo!"

He chuckles and I hear phlegm stirring in his throat as his laughter continues. He playfully slaps a hand on my shoulder. Despite the spearmint gum, his breath smells faintly of alcohol. "You're fair lookin', see, I'll help you out. Where are ya—ahhh!" He jumps back theatrically when he sees my hand. "Whaddid yuh do to yaself, love?"

I do not realize that I have been smiling the entire time this cab driver was speaking to me until I look back at my hand and feel a smile disappear from my face. "Oh it's minor, really. Just a slash over the knuckle but I'm afraid I need a couple stitches."

"A couple? You're bleedin' all over the place!"

"No, no it looks worse than it is, I think. Where's the closest hospital with an emergency room? Will you take me?"

He moves around the car with a cumbersome trudge and opens the passenger door for me. "Yeah, yeah, get on in. The closest 'ospital is St. Vincent's."

He walks with a bit of a limp but I do not mind, just like I do not mind his minty booze breath. By the time we are both settled in the car, the Jaguar and Mercedes parked in front of us have driven away with their evening prizes. The cab driver clears his throat and sings to me again, "Young lady, how how hoowwwwwww did you hurt your hannnndddddd?"

So maybe I shouldn't be in a car in a foreign country with a bloody hand and an intoxicated middle-aged man, but he has such a lovely voice I can't help it. "Oh it's such a stupid story. I wish I could say I punched somebody in the face but really I just broke a glass washing dishes."

"Ah ha! You can still say you punched somebody if that's what you want to say! You ever done that before, anyway? Where are you from? America, right?"

"Yes, Vermont. I go to school here for now, though."

"Ver-mont? Up by Canada? Gets cold up there!"

He sings an unfamiliar tune about icy streets and chilly air. His accent is thick and I cannot make out all the lyrics but I am entertained. He keeps his eyes on the road but is polite enough to keep eye contact with me at stop lights. He looks at me as he sings this winter song and then stops abruptly to say, "Uh doo dah karaoke qui' well, love."

"What's that about karaoke?"

"I do the karaoke quite well, don't I, love?"

"Ahh! Of course! Do you go often?"

"Often? Always! And all over too! I was in London last week singing with some of me old friends. I'd known them since I was young. They're mostly my brother's friends. But we're all old now so it doesn't matter." He slaps the steering wheel and laughs loudly. "Actually went to America with a couple of 'em once. A few years back."

"What part of America?"

"New York, which was just grand of course, just wonderful. I loved it. Loved it. Would live there if I had the money but who does?" He laughs hysterically again. "What's that song New York has for itself?"

"A song?"

"Oh you know the New York, Neww Yoorrrrkkk." He sings Frank Sinatra's "New York, New York."

I laugh and clap softly with my fragile hand. "Where else did you venture to while you were in the States?"

"Oh I've been all over there. Never to Vermont but I've been to Boston, California, Myrtle Beach—is that what you call it? Uh, D.C. Washington D.C.! You been there, I'm sure."

"Definitely. I live only a few hours from there. I…."

"Did you go to the inauguration then?!"

"No, no—I was here, actually. I've been here since January but I watched it on TV."

"Ah, he's a breath of fresh air, isn't he? What do yuh think of him? You vote for 'im?"

"He is a breath of fresh air. And a captivating speaker. I mean I voted for him but I'm not really into being a fan of particular politicians, so I'm not as enthusiastic as everybody else, but…."

"Oh right, right. Usually they're all shit. You know about any over here? Most of 'em shit."

"I'm afraid I only know a few names but I'm not as familiar with Ireland's politics as I should be."

"Ah, that's okay. America is so big anyhow, but that's the problem with it. Americans don't know anything about anyone except themselves."

It's true. I want him to keep talking, to tell me everything I am supposed to know even if he is ignorant too but he is waiting for me to speak. "I know. It's awful really, I don't even know enough about my own country. And America is so isolated too. I...."

"Ah, to shit with it. That's okay! Dublin's America's 51st state anyhow. Ninety-nine percent of Dublin will love Americans even if they aren't too bright."

Oh, what a charming man, trying to justify my ignorance. I appreciate it, really, but I still feel like a failure. "Really? I've been welcome here thus far, but I didn't know Dublin had such a high opinion of America."

"Oh, why not? Of course. You ever seen that episode of the Simpsons on St. Paddy's Day?"

"Yes, I have actually! Ha!"

"Ah, the Irish love that. All the Americans getting into St. Paddy's and all. It's tacky and dumb but it's great!" He laughs. Then coughs. "And do you remember, well, you were young but Clinton came over here and he was great to Ireland. Great."

"I remember seeing something about it on TV but I'm afraid I can't recall any details."

"Ah, well, like I said, you're young. But trust me when I say, America is great, don't you worry about it. You're not worried are yuh? Yuh look worried." He laughs loudly and heartily yet again. Nothing is funny but I laugh too because I'm happy right now.

"I'm not worried. About America. Or Ireland. I like it here."

He looks at my hand and scowls. "Maybe you should be a little worried, eh?" He chuckles softly as if all his previous laughter has made him tired. 'Ospital is right up here. I'm only gonna charge you seven euro, okay?"

"Oh, okay, thank you. Thank you very much."

The cab pulls up to the emergency room entrance. I pay the driver seven euro. He watches me dig through my wallet for the right amount of change pathetically, with my left hand. He is breathing heavily. I can smell the boozy mint odor again mixed with the scent of the cab's leather seat and part of me hopes I never find the right amount of change because I like this smell and I want to stay a part of it. And as much as I have gotten to know this man for such a short cab ride, I don't nearly know enough.

I hand him seven euro and a little extra, and I notice the giddiness in his eyes has faded. He gives me a nod and a smile—one of those simple smiles that just requires a tuck in of the upper lip, one of those smiles that people feel obligated to give. I don't expect such a gesture from this jubilant man and I suddenly wonder if he felt obligated to put on such a production for me during the car ride. He didn't have to. I hope he did that because he wanted to, because that is who he really is. I don't know why I care so much anyway. I don't know him. "Where are you headed after this?"

"Ahh, ladyyyyy laaaaaddddddyyyyy," he sings, "haven't you learned anything about Ireland?"

I'm tentative. I open my mouth to speak even though I do not know what I am going to say and luckily, he speaks for me.

"I'm headed to the pub! I told yuh I've been off duty for a while!" He slaps the steering wheel again and wheezes through his laughter.

The stinging pain in my hand that disappeared during the drive has returned but I smile anyway. "Good," I say. "Very good."

Breaking Concrete

John R. Gunther

My father picked up his beer. Drank some. We were eating lunch on the front porch. We had been breaking up the old concrete sidewalk that ran the length of the side yard out to the front porch. My mother wanted a new flagstone walk put in and I had volunteered. The work was brutal. I broke the concrete by wielding a sledgehammer like the mighty Thor. "For Asgard!" I shouted. And then had to explain the reference.

"Get that from some religion course?"

"Nope, comic book."

He smiled. "Comic book. Well, you always did like that stuff."

We levered the pieces up with crowbars. Slammed them into a wheelbarrow and carted the fractured walkway to a dumpsite out back. The mailman came into the yard. He had worked with my father and I had gone to school with his son. He saw what we were doing.

"Just the two of you?" he asked. "Remind me to never mess with either of you."

Now, my father stared across the road at the Phillips' house where a pickup game of basketball was in raucous progress. He drank some more. Stared longer at the basketball game.

"Did I ever tell you about the time your grandfather pulled me right out of a basketball game that I was playing in high school?"

He took another sip. Put the bottle down on the porch railing. Instantly, he snatched the bottle back up. Placed a rag on the railing and put the bottle on top of the rag. "The son of a bitch pulled me right out of the fucking game."

What was this? I had never heard my father use that word. I had been told that my father had been a star player in any sport he chose. I had heard the stories and was inclined to dismiss them as the typical aging jock war tales. The truth was that the stories were understated. After researching newspaper articles and listening to his buddies, I realized that he was the real thing. When I was sixteen and he was fifty-four, we were swimming together in the lake. He was teaching me this stroke that he had made up when he worked at a summer resort during his teenage years. He matched me stroke for stroke.

"It was halftime," he said. "The game was a bitch. This team we were playing was goddamned good. Fast little shits. Took everything we could throw at them. The game was real close—maybe two points difference. So here we were in the locker room at halftime. Worried and anxious—not talking. Then in walks your grandfather. He points to me. 'Junior, hit the shower. You're out of the game.'

"I was stunned. The place got even quieter. 'Dad, what are you doing? What's going on?'

"'Nice try,' he said. 'I found your last report card. Your mother tried to hide it. We had this talk before. You don't study, you don't play. Take a shower and get dressed.'

"The coach couldn't believe what was happening. 'Jesus Christ, Paul, why don't you just cut all of our throats while you're at it? In case you haven't noticed, Paul Junior here is our best player.'

"'Sorry, George, he's out. There is no discussion.'

"Problem was, I knew he was right. Didn't make it any better. Took about four days before the two of us spoke civilly to each other. Yeah, right out of the fucking game."

He drained the last of his beer. "The game," he muttered.

Symbiosis/Parasitosis

Jaime Berry

i.

I walked into the cafeteria swearing that today I wouldn't be such a pussy.

I walked into the cafeteria strangling my gloves and thinking that if I just asked, if he just said yes, everything would be perfect; life would be perfect. I was thinking about the trip to the Caribbean we'd had; I was thinking about that day we'd made love on the forest floor and all the leaves I'd taken home in my hair. I was thinking that he and I had had three hundred and sixty-two days as lovers before I'd ended it. I was thinking I had made a mistake. I was thinking about making it right.

I sat down. I looked at him. I opened my mouth, and shut it. Turns out, I really am a pussy.

Not you, though. You're the kind of woman who takes what she wants.

You sat up, turned, and caught my "good morning" with your lips.

Your mouth met mine for an entire second. Just long enough for me to realize what was happening, just long enough to make me confused and just the slightest bit giddy. Just long enough for me to enjoy it without thinking it through.

I hardly knew you, but I already knew it was your kind of move.

It's strange how life can be tragic and beautiful all at once. Your grandmother had died. But I believe a little in God now because she gave me the rest of my life. She gave me you.

ii.

The first time you told me you loved me, you followed immediately with, "Tell me why?"

On the other end of the phone, I was terrified of giving you the wrong answer. I told you because I listened, because I was gentle with you. I whispered, because I might be just a little bit beautiful.

You told me I was right. I trembled for the next hour. I don't know if I was still afraid or excited.

iii.

Do you know how many times during a phone call you just sound annoyed, you tell me to shut up in not so many words? Do you know how little your voice gets soft and sincere these days? It's our second winter and you haven't forgotten New England out there in California; your heart's at forty below.

Sometimes I want to shake you, want to do x-rays and biopsies and make sure your voice box is still working because you tell me you love me in the same tone you talk to me about cereal.

iv.

My father used to be a Boy Scout. He liked to be prepared; he hid spare keys.

In my father's living room, we sat naked on the floor by the coffee table, feeding each other sushi with chopsticks. We were both a little clumsy. I bought the spicy kind because I knew they were your favorite, and you left the California rolls for me because you knew I wouldn't eat anything else. I poured you apple juice and passed you the glass over a bouquet of miniature roses.

It was the most romantic thing I'd ever done.

Later, in my childhood bed, we made love. I dragged those little roses over your skin in the failing light, kneeled on the carpet and just watched you move. You didn't know that I'd lain here the night you called crying; you didn't know I'd paced here the night you went missing. Your eyes were closed and you were remembering all the roses I'd ever bought.

And that's what I wanted.

v.

I counted; we'd been together one year and forty-three days. It had been thirty-seven days since I'd seen you, and you were sleeping with someone else. I promised you could fuck whoever you wanted, but I never meant for you to be with someone exactly like me in all the most important ways.

I'm afraid he doesn't have my flaws. I'm afraid that's going to matter.

When I closed my eyes, all I could see was you crawling across the sheets, touching his skin with fingers that would make him feel electric. I fell asleep telling myself over and over that he doesn't mean a thing, but you'd do it over and over until you could see the prints of your bodies in the mattress, until the scent of your hair was stuck in his pillow.

It's not a secret, but I almost wished it was.

vi.

I arrived on your doorstep in the middle of a blizzard in a T-shirt and sandals, clutching my keys in one hand, and a windshield wiper in the other. My only explanation was that I had to see you.

You smiled and said, "It's okay. I had to see you too."

In your bedroom, we slow danced across all the available floor. You danced on your toes so you could sing in my ear, so I could feel the melody in your breath across my skin.

We waltzed in ellipses for hours, to your voice, to the wind. When we finally stopped, my heart stopped, too; you looked at me like I was the most beautiful thing on the face of the Earth.

vii.

Making love to you makes me feel immortal.

viii.

You'd been gone five weeks the first time I slept with somebody else; you'd spent thirty-four days in uniform, training to invade, to kill, and you were holding a gun the first time I slept with somebody else.

He held my hand when he took me to our bed, kissed all the right places. He touched all the parts of me you sometimes forgot, and when I touched him he whispered my name like I was something holy.

I'm not; I wasn't and I wanted him to leave and take the lies with him.

But I was already naked. I'd already said yes with my eyes and my hips and my fingertips and I was afraid my mouth couldn't take it back.

Halfway between his orgasm and the one I faked, I was staring at the ceiling and wishing you were there. You were two thousand miles away holding a gun, and I was wishing you were there instead because your trigger finger could have been the voice of reason.

Bang. Like a firework.

It would have made more sense than when he said my name like that.

ix.

You forgot your Vicodin.

I didn't know to remind you.

It rained. Our breath crawled over the glass in bursts of steam, clouding the view of trees, my neighbor's house, and the county jail.

I cooked you mashed potatoes, pressed my hands to the glass till my fingers froze, drew you a heart with the tip of my nose just to hear you laugh.

Your skin was hot like the outside of a mug. I pressed my palms to your belly, willing the cold to combat the cramps that might make you faint. I rested my lips against your ear and whispered you fairytales no one else would ever hear: the nugget prince, the mashed potato princess.

"… And they all lived, and ate, happily ever after."

x.

Witness—testimony.

You love me with your fingers and your eyes, with the curve of your back. You love me with your toes. You love me in the middle of the night, when your lashes flutter, when you smile in your sleep, when you move into my caresses. You love me in the morning, when the first thing you do is say good morning to my lips, with yours. You love me in the afternoon, when we're making love for lunch, when we're weaving food-filled fairytales—on your off days.

Witness—the telephone.

We cannot touch: no fingers or eyes or curves of any kind. No toes. No lashes fluttering, no smiles, no caresses. Just goodnight. No lips, no silent movements. Just morning. Sweetie. No making love, no cold hands or feet or fingers.

No fairytales anymore.

…Guilty, guilty, guilty…

Aren't we all?

But you, so much more than I expected.

xi.

You have this incredible ability to always make me the bad guy, to always make me feel like I've fucked up no matter what really happened.

I'm not so concerned with the how. I know how. I used to be so good at that.

I just wonder why.

xii.

I'm falling backward faster than your eyes can follow.

xiii.

Why can't anyone read between the lines anymore?

Telling you I need you would be so selfish. It would inconvenience you. It would be doing something for me.

I take so much better care of your life than I do mine.

xiv.

You were coughing so hard I actually looked up your doctor's on-call phone number; I put 911 on speed dial.

I went to Wal-Mart, but I couldn't buy you cough syrup because I couldn't prove I was over eighteen. I bought you decongestants instead, three packages, and a humidifier. I bought you lozenges and Vicks Vapor Rub and herbal remedies; I bought you vitamins. I rented seven different comedies and tucked you into bed with a thermometer and chamomile tea, rocked you in my lap and sang you lullabies until you fell asleep.

It was just a little after seven.

At three in the morning, you woke me up with kisses, trailing your chapped lips over my neck, my shoulder. In a hoarse whisper, you begged me to love you, to make love to you.

How could I refuse?

In the dancing blue light of late-night television I kissed every last inch of your skin; I murmured poetry into your hips, your thighs; I traced my name in your collarbones, stroked fairytales into your spine. You were a goddess in all that flickering light, and I worshipped your body with mine.

When you came down from the high of your orgasm you could hardly move. I moved you gently, like a doll, raising and bending your limbs to get you back in your clothes. I leaned your torso against mine to pull your shirt over your head, and you protested, weakly, your fingers trembling with exhaustion against my ribs.

"I want your skin."

xv.

I sat up long nights at the beach, digging holes in the sand that I could sink into, watching the tide come in. I knew that you were looking at the ocean too, but one of us had to be looking at the wrong one because my hands were both empty and my heart didn't feel any better.

Waiting for the water to hit my shoes, I traced constellations to look like your face, and wrote our names in the stars.

… Did you see?

xvi.

My chest, my arms, my hands are all so tired of this tension, of the lack of attention. All of a sudden my vital pieces become invisible and nobody noticed.

Aren't people supposed to applaud when the magician disappears? Oh appearances. You said you'd never notice. You didn't. You don't. At least you kept your word.

xvii.

One is an isolated hour. I cover my ears while the floors squeal,
the refrigerator hums, the heater groans. I hold my breath. Anything
is better than answering my conscience, letting my fingers touch
the flaws hiding in my pocket, making eye contact with the mistake
hiding in the next room. I bite my lip, try not to call out for a lover
I'm afraid will never answer.

The TV is the only light in this entire house, and I'm thinking of
turning it out.

xviii.

We were one hour and forty-seven minutes into 2008 and we'd
been together for sixty-three days.

You didn't know it, but my New Year's resolution was to love myself the way you loved me.

We were lying nose to nose in the mansion chair, and all I could
see in the dark were your eyes. More than anything I wanted to
know what you could be thinking to turn your eyes that particular
shade of amber around the edges, to brighten that starburst of sienna.

I didn't ask out loud. But you answered anyway. "Will you marry
me?"

I hadn't thought about it. I hadn't thought about us beyond
tomorrow, beyond next week; I hadn't thought about apartments or
rings or pets. I hadn't thought about children. I hadn't thought about
shared closets or cooking or paying bills; I hadn't thought about
which drawer we should put the silverware in.

It didn't matter. We could fight about dogs later, or baby names;
we could worry about laundry detergent and joint checking and floor
plans six years from now, or sixty. I couldn't be without you.

"Yes. Yes, baby."

xix.

There's so much to tell you. But where, and when, and how? How can I explain that he slept in boxers and I slept in jeans, and the particular way in which his heartbeat differs from yours did not entirely bother me? How do I explain that I feel misinformed, suddenly a part of this couple that has known (always known), this couple that has reason to sleep on the same sheets and smile in the morning? How do I explain that I'm sleeping with someone else and that the guilt I feel is only mild, that the guilt has no effect on the way he makes me laugh or how our bodies fit together.

How do I tell you what it costs? In the sunlight I can replace my childhood with someone else's; I become the product of sledding and Barbie dolls and home-cooked meals. But in the early morning, I remember myself with a startling clarity. The light fades, and suddenly my childhood is my own again, suddenly I am composed of consequences, of another person's mistakes. I curl up in a corner and sob over all the boys since the first, all the choices I let him influence: all the groping mouths and greedy hands and acquiescence, all the nudity. In between all those moments I can never understand why I did what I did.

xx.

I'm all tears and blotches, hair falling out in clumps, skin cracked to bleeding, lip splitting in two.

I'm a mess.

And you, letting a boy (you say) you don't even love keep you from doing what makes you happy.

What have you done with the woman I love?

What happened to me? To you?

What happened to us?

xxi.

I lied.

I don't miss you constantly; I haven't missed you every moment since I saw you last.

I used to. But I can't anymore.

When I catch myself, I feel this insane satisfaction, this thrill in knowing that even if you aren't thinking about me, sometimes I'm not thinking about you either.

I could be anywhere, you know; I could be at home or I could be in Cleveland, Ohio, making shower drains; I could be in Chicago studying art or I could be painting in Oakland.

I could be right fucking next to you and what would it matter?

Years from now, when we're married, and we have a big beautiful house, I still won't be enough for you. You'll meet someone, just out on the street, at the takeout place on your way home. (You're like that—you meet people everywhere; you'd meet people in the middle of nowhere). He'll ask you out; he'll ask for your number and you'll hesitate.

You'll hesitate but you'll say no. You'll come home to me. You'll make love to me and you'll be happy; you'll curl up in my arms and fall asleep. But on those nights when you're left awake, when I'm curled up sleeping on the sheets next to you, you won't be happy. You'll lie there with the TV on, volume turned down until it buzzes in your ears, watching the lights on the ceiling, thinking about all the places that you could be tonight if you didn't have to be here with me.

xxii.

You called today at four thirty-two AM. I'd been asleep for nearly twelve minutes and I thought the ringing was my alarm.

I answered, "Snooze. Shut up."

You replied, "Okay. But I love you. Really." And hung up.

[four]

The Self

You Have To

Ashley DeFelice

You have to skip breakfast. If you start eating that early, when you're not even really hungry yet, your day's pretty much wrecked. Luckily, it's easy to feel strong in the morning. It's the best time to plan the day's food. A can of soup's always good, or so is a little mug of strawberry granola. If you want to splurge, you can plan on having half a chocolate bar, but then you've got to remember that you can't have anything else till the next day.

Make sure when you go to school that you don't bring a coat, food, or money. Being cold burns calories, and then by the time school's halfway over, you're gonna be hungry. It'll be frustrating and your hands will probably shake, but it'll be worth it. When it's really hard, remember that by not eating in front of everyone else, that's probably making you seem less fat.

Try not to think too much about food during math. If you do, you'll just keep thinking about it more and more until the thought gets stuck in your head and you devour everything as soon as you get home. Think about anything else. Even try thinking about math, if you can bear it. If you can't, try comparing the other kids to you. Are their collarbones more obvious than yours? Are their stomachs perfectly flat? Can you make your stomach perfectly flat if you really try? Try.

Do the same thing on the bus home. It's easier on the bus because you can hang out with your friends and whisper about the creepy homeless people sitting across from you, but you're so close to getting to eat that it might be hard anyway.

Have your meal as soon as you get home, so you have an excuse for skipping supper. If your parents start bugging you about nutrition, do your best to ignore them. They might tell you that you look fine the way you are, or that you're getting too skinny, but you have to remember that because they're your parents, they're basically obligated to say you look beautiful, and that has nothing to do with the reality.

How to Teach Your Fourteen-Year-Old Daughter to Drive

Christina Etre

1. Start by rummaging through the coolers at your parents' Christmas Eve party. Take a beer. Complain that it's Heineken, but drink it anyway.
2. Move on to margaritas. You don't normally drink them, but your brother, Stephen, is making them for everybody—he always does when he's in town. Give a few to your wife, too. They're her favorite.
3. Lose track of your seventeen-year-old son. Let him sneak into the basement and drink something questionable with his cousins. He's not drunk; he's just embracing the Christmas spirit.
4. Let your brother, Jim, convince you to consume a few Jell-O shots.
5. Watch your wife paint the fingernails of two of your passed-out brothers. People are falling asleep—it's time to head home.
6. Stumble out the front door and step right into a bucket of melting ice and empty bottles. Narrowly avoid falling on your face as you remove your wet shoe.
7. Hold your shoe in your right hand as you stare at your family. Decide not to drive.
8. Ask your wife to drive. When she says she can't, ask your son.
9. Look at him with disgust when he says he can't.
10. Ask some other family members to drive you home. They're drunker than you.
11. Put your fourteen-year-old daughter in the driver's seat.
12. Apologize to her.
13. Move the seat up a few inches.
14. Tell her to ease onto the gas. Don't let her go over twenty-five miles per hour.
15. Hold onto one side of the wheel.

16. Gasp roughly 17 times—or just every time you see another car.
17. Apologize every few feet.
18. Don't talk about it the next day.

To Be A Wildflower

Marissa Caan

I went hiking and picked some wildflowers for my mother. She told me they were the kind that opened during the day and closed at night. When I saw petals in retreat on her bedside table, I wondered how flowers know to open and close at the appropriate time.

It's raining, a damp November. I am on a train to New York City. I look out the window, and the bricks blur into a frame of wet paint. Sometimes you move so fast that you don't even feel like you are moving at all.

The first time I saw you was through hookah smoke. Sitting on an orange jungle gym in Riverside Park that glowed in the light of dusk, until it was completely dark and we could only see charcoal outlines of each other. You spoke with odd inflections that filled space in the humid air. *You look uncomfortable.* I was looking over your head, not into your eyes.

You printed a black and white picture of Lenin at the library and hung it over your bed with blue masking tape.

The sheets came off my bed, and our bare legs twisted on plastic. Our clothes were wet from the rain, but they sat in a pile, your socked feet feeling damp against my skin. *What do you think love is?* I don't remember what I said; I knew where you were going. *Love is affection.* You wrapped your arms around me. When you tried to kiss me on the steps before class, I was embarrassed and held my breath.

Eyes as wide as saucers, plain brown like grainless wood. A birthmark near your tear duct.

The stairwell of a hotel in Times Square. Lights buzz. I see your armpit hair as you reach up to grab something from a pipe. A metal tag with an etched number. It's good luck. You illustrate with a story I can't remember. I throw it off the side of my backyard later when I realize it isn't, into the gutter filled with overgrown brush.

You ran through headlight beams. No shirt on, your torso was a V. Arms wrapped around a boom box playing rap from the Bay; I threw my arms up in the air. *I always smile when I think of you, always so cheerful, getting so hyphy.* When we walked into the grocery store across the street, I asked you to turn off the music.

Muggy heat pours into the city like plumes of smoke. We are walking away from the Natural History Museum, hand in hand. The leaves are wet like sweating skin. I try to walk ahead. But you, you have nowhere to be.

The wet air made me sick. Your suggestion was whiskey. I laughed so that it was a joke.

My sister is arriving at Penn Station. Friday afternoon. Gloomy and restless. The city swells. We force our way onto the downtown train, slithering in the crevices between sticky bodies. You are able to grab onto the metal pole but there is nothing for me to hold on to. I lean up against you with my back turned, and grab onto the side of your thighs. I brace as we lurch. A few seconds later you laugh, ashamed. You are fifteen, still a boy who stands with his hands in front of his body.

I knock on your door three times for you to let me in. You stick your head out of the crack between the door and the frame, and I can tell the room behind you is dark. You open the door slowly, just like the way you lifted up your pants to show me burns on your knees from wrestling on carpet.

I am in this room for the rest of the summer. My feet grind rose petals into the floor. There is a bouquet of red roses on your bed.

Freshly cut and wrapped in pink plastic. I rest my neck in the corner of your shoulder and breathe in your skin because I think this is romance.

You have ten condoms lined up perfectly in your desk drawer. I pick the one that glows in the dark.

You are stark naked and
waiting for me—
olive, wet skin,
black hair on your breastbone.
body tapered,
a trapezoid.
Hands that expand
and reach for the ground
through my hipbones.
For now,
I only feel it there.

As I walk down the hallway, the boys stand under their door frames, watching my legs float by. Tomorrow, you get pats on your back, firm like wood, and I pretend like I don't see. For your first time, you fucked a drunk girl. Upstairs at a house party in Berkeley.

When I wrote about it in that cold room with a green chalkboard, I put my arm around my notebook and folded the page like an elementary school girl.

Daryl came back from a weekend in Maine and saw dead flowers on my desk. She later told me she then knew exactly what had happened.

You wanted to take advantage of the empty room. Someone came

to take a picture after we left. My hair was wispy and tangled as I
walked ahead of you towards the elevator.
Vaspetabuk and Samuel. *Rolls right off the tongue.* The name of the
novel you started. *I've had those names in my head for years.* I pictured
myself finding it in the sale bin at a bookstore. *One day, you can say
you were my muse the summer I started writing it.* I read the first eighteen pages. *It's about this boy Samuel whose father dies, so he goes into
the wilderness to find his grandfather. He's just a lost kid.* Your middle
name is Samuel.

We spent that night in subways. Waiting for the train, I imagined
grass. Sticking to my legs. You lying next to me, your breath like
wind. Instead, it was the gust of hot air that blew my hair as the
train we wanted pulled away.

*I hope you had the patience to wait and read this until you at least
arrived in the airport. You know I love you, Marissa, and I am going to
miss you. But nothing is forever, and we're only five hours apart. Don't
get too emotional!*

The day after I got home from New York was my birthday. I went to
see a movie with my mother and turned off my phone. *Never pay for
movies, that's what I say.* I turned it back on and you still hadn't called.
It was four in the afternoon. The library was giving away a book
of Borges's short stories. I picked it up because I remembered you
talking about him. That night before bed, I opened the book to the
last story, "The South." *I know that the next few weeks of waiting will
be a bit shitty for me, but I'll make up for it once I'm on Highway Five,
racing my way south.* I can see you with the windows open and country music leaving no echo, only a path of dust. Your hand tapping the
wheel, the sky burning. Needless to say, you never came. You stayed
up North where it was cool.

I miss you and I love you.
Three days go by.
I miss you and I love ya.
I knew things were over.
I walk up and down the hills in Chinatown. Bodies colliding like a
stuck zipper. Later, I sit in a square with my head hung in between
my knees. My back forms a bay of air instead of water, hollow.
Waiting for a call that was caught in the San Francisco air.

There is a half moon between my hips and the car when you come
through the haze wearing a cowboy hat. You have dirt under your
fingernails and grime on your face. You are driving cross-country in
an old Suburban running on vegetable oil. We both have bright eyes
in the afternoon sun.
I make sure to walk with a sway. Your eyes follow me like lasers,
making thick red lines until I sit down. *I forgot.* Forgot what? *Forgot
how good it was to be with you.* You get up. My eyes make lines too.
In the elevator you stand facing me. Hands clasped in front of your
body. My back in the corner, against a steel railing. Between us, only
a few footsteps, a pregnant distance. But we are falling, and air tun-
nels in that space. The doors open and shut again. We walk side by
side as I dig for my car keys.
When I try to define the word "regret," this is what I come up with:

From behind, you kiss me on the cheek and call me "Sweetie." We
are at a baseball game. I smell your neck, freckled, pressing my nose
into your collarbone. But this is the dream I have a year later. I remember the bar you took me to after a Yankees game. Floors sticky
with wax and humid air. You called me "Sweetie" when you asked if I
wanted a glass of water, and ordered yourself a beer.

It is March now and you call me again. *Just passing through LA on
my way back from San Diego. 150 miles past LA on the Five. What was*

that song you used to always sing, you know, "I ain't got no money"? It starts ringing through the phone. *I graduated in January and was a restaurant manager and I trained and hired people. People with degrees from Berkeley, and I wasn't even out of high school. But you, how are you doing? I'm happy. You could sound happier. I am happy. You should come up to Berkeley for spring break!* I have plans. *LA is an armpit, I know.* You don't know LA. *Altadena, Long Beach, all different areas...* You know shit. My voice is harsh and cold when I say goodbye. You are
an echo in the hills.
Lost but resounding.
I drive Mulholland with Leah. We talk about the time last year when we stopped in an empty lot on the ridge and screamed. She reminds me that I was screaming about you. Hoping you would drift away along highways like veins. I thought I could see where that would take you, to the ends of the city, clear in the distance. But tonight, with the windows closed, your name is stagnant in the air. I drive this road like a razor, unable to see its curves as the hills fade
into night.

[five]

The Self in the World

DEPENDING

Alexa Ercolano

Depending on whether or not we had
        eaten well that day, we could participate
            in the four o'clock walk. One of the nurses
                would gather us together—both eating and
                    mood disorder patients—and we would
                        head outside; for some of us, it would
                        be for the first time in days. There was always
                    weird electricity buzzing through the group,
                a mixture of excitement and apprehension.
        We looked different from the rest of the
    businessmen and medical students on
    the street, and because of this we stood
out a lot. Together we would shuffle
down the dirty East Baltimore sidewalk, a nervous
    clump of the mentally disturbed funneling
        through crowds of people who had
            it a little more together than we.

            During one of these walks, I ran into an under-
            classman from my high school. We made eye
            contact and there was a flicker of recognition
            across his face, but then he saw my hospital
            wristband and my companions, and suddenly
            looked confused.

            I hurried by him and kept my head low
            for the rest of the walk.

Man Up

Christian Belekewicz

When I'm worn out, everything feels more daunting and I feel less
able to handle it. I get overwhelmed easily, especially around loud
noises. I feel social or adventurous only when I'm at peak health, and
I seldom feel like I'm reaching that. Whether that's due to actual
physical issues or just mental ones is another story. I always hoped
I had some weird disease to explain this condition, and that one
day the doctor would find it in a blood test and ask me, "How did
you make it this far without treatment?" That would be a relief as
opposed to the obvious answer: fear and depression, or worse,
inadequacy as a human being.

But midsummer was aging; the nights grew cooler, sliding down
the tipping point of the solstice. It was time to buck up and make
up for all those days just sitting idly on the porch, drenched in heat,
not being able to keep a clear head. I supposed that was my logic for
forcing myself to go along with my old friend Andy. Maybe it would
lead to a good time, and I tried to forget the fact that once I got into
Andy's truck, there was no going back if it led somewhere I didn't
want to be. I finished a beer through halfhearted mouthfuls, trying
not to gag like I do when I get nervous.

I wish I'd been more forthright about what I was willing to put up
with. We made a stop at a lonely one-story house in some neighborhood I'd never been to off Old County Road because Andy needed
to get weed. Whatever, I'd wait in the car. A half hour passes and
I can see him through the window talking to someone's mother
with emphatic hand gestures, wielding those massive pale plumber
hands, liberally applying broad smiles to every remark. I get out of
the car and walk down a few houses to take a piss. There are no trees
separating these yards and everybody keeps their lights on all night,
maybe to feel safe or more alive, teeming with significance. I would

be easily spotted if most people weren't watching TV.

I look up at the stars forming gleaming pirouettes in the sky. We don't get this often during the humid Cape Cod summer months. I call my friend Dave who owns a telescope, with whom I play music at night and sit outside for hours watching the stars while I talk his ear off about life beyond Earth. He's out of town.

Andy finally comes back out. I ask him what the fuck took so long but can't really catch the answer because of the way he talks, low-pitched, nasal, and fast-mumbling. The details don't matter to me anyway. It's something you just sort of blurt out because you're frustrated.

Andy gets a sudden case of lead foot and now we're driving ninety in a thirty on a battered lumpy road that has cracked apart and been glued back together again. I have Deftones blasting on the radio with piercing treble, screaming along to the music, which smoothly transitioned into screaming at him.

"OKAY! OKAY! FOR FUCK'S SAKE, ANDY!" I press my feet into the floor like there's a brake pedal there. He turns down the music and laughs like Goofy. Any one of these side streets could have a cop car tucked away in them, waiting like a nighttime predator for the right moment to pounce.

"You realize that was, like, pull-guns-on-you-and-arrest-you-on-the-spot fast, right?" he asks.

"That makes sense."

"Cause I mean they basically just expect a fuckin' lunatic to be behind the wheel, y'know?"

I should've known I'd end up here. Sean Gallagher's. Gal was one of the figureheads of the in-crowd in high school, which from my peripheral vantage point appeared to be subdivided into two sects, the preps and the more thuggish. Gal represented the latter, the nucleus of one of the two atoms that formed the overarching molecule of coolness. I think I was in chemistry when I came up with that analogy. So while the prep group split off to pursue business, marketing, or economics careers at oversized universities, the other guys decided to stick around for a while and wait for "alternate avenues of opportunity" that never actually passed through town, but by the time it was obvious, they had probably already forgotten they had been waiting in the first place.

There was a plethora of alibis to draw from, used in conversations with friends' parents who happened to ask what they were doing with their lives, but I think they may all boil down to one truth, which was somewhere among the empty beer cans and bottles, the tacky floor, the blaring rap, and the weathered, moss-eaten porch where everyone smoked cigarettes and scrapped to release pent up frustration.

I didn't mind stopping in once in a while. Ry, Savoy, Tallia, Big Dan, Conor Carroll, some other guys like that. A lot of them went by their last names. Then there was Andy, who had been more a part of my ragtag outsider group, acquainted with many but close with only a few. He had been involved with this group recently, while others were away at school, something to occupy time during the desolate Cape winters. In the summers when he wasn't on his hands and knees fixing pipes indoors he was at the beach day-drinking and going to the tanning booth to compensate for his pasty skin.

I had a scant but recognizable history with this group, from back when we all snowballed cars and smoked mini cigars before rinsing with mouthwash to hide the smell, to years later when I awkwardly stood around at Friday night house parties, giving the occasional head nod and 'sup" salutation. These shit shows were an unspoken mandate if you wanted to be anybody.

I sat at the table in the kitchen, shuffling a deck of cards, watching them take shots. Gal was walking around with his chest out and a tattered baseball cap pulled over his already-receding hairline, clutching a plastic cup full of ice and liquor in one hand and chaser in the other. Bottoms up. My insides were churning. Most of the time I only drink like that when I'm at home. Gal slams his cup down on the flimsy wood table. "Let's go to the fuckin' strip club!"

I wish I had more money. With a ten-dollar surcharge just to gain access to even more expensive debauchery, Zachary's is the only strip club on Cape Cod, and isn't featured in any of the tourist brochures with sunset beach shots on the covers. It's in the town of Mashpee, right on the side of the main road, and during the day you can see a bucket truck holding up the American flag and a red Budweiser big rig out front. When I was young and we would drive past, my parents would tell me that it was just a restaurant with really bad food, which is why we would never go there when I asked.

Mashpee is the home of the renowned Willowbend Country Club and golf course, and is one of the poorest towns on Cape. It's also an old Wampanoag stomping ground, but I don't think there's much pure blood or tradition around anymore. There's only one powwow a year, advertised with handwritten picket signs on the rotary. We once joked that if we went to one of these things, the Native Americans would dance around our car, and when the crowd dissipated, it would be up on cinder blocks. In all seriousness, I don't blame them for such a thing. There is undoubtedly a connection between sprawling golf courses, trendy shopping plazas, and underprivileged neighborhoods suggesting lost culture.

Zach's is a brick building with blacked-out windows. There's an older man in front of me in line with slicked gray hair pulled back and a wife or girlfriend with skin too old for her tight skimpy dress, but good for her for being comfortable with herself. The old man says something, grinning to the guys behind him and they laugh and pat him on the back. Burly men in tight black tees examine my ID.

And suddenly sore sights and smells are all around me, but it's exhilarating and it's right there, black felt floors, the polished wood stage and poles, green and pink neon lights lining everything and reflecting off the metal bar counter. You can see the speakers shake with the bass line and the girls, of course, the girls wearing exactly what you'd imagine, waiting on drunken, aroused customers, sad men from hollow homes getting old looking to find that niche of pleasure in their lives, the last spark before they can't feel much at all. Some are riding a lazy river on pension, bored out of their minds, and some are eagerly chasing that big break that will leave them wishing they took that trip to another country when they were younger. Other men here are tourists who trailered their three-seat jet skis around back, with sun-burnt shaved heads and useless glamour muscles, looking to get their kicks for the night. Looking to get pussy. PUSSY.

The dancers get to brass tacks, providing little element of mystery. Many of them just come out topless right from the start, while others use the string of their top as a place for fingers to prod bills into. I watch my friend Ry place a few dollars onto the rope around the stage, as if he could've just as well done nothing. He's a good looking guy, masculine, but with this quirky copper hair and a personality to match. He could never quite take anything in life seriously, and I think that's why I always liked him more than the others. He was willing to step back from the drama and muse over absurdities. The dancer approaches him on all fours, clad in what looks like a tribal loin cloth. She closes in and wraps her legs around his head, dangling her vagina in front of him like an anglerfish. He stares with a bemused smirk on his face. I'm howling from a booth in the back.

"Excuse me, no phones or cameras sir." A pudgy man with bulging eyes leans over to me. I don't make trouble and try for conversation.

"Are you Irish? Your voice sounds Irish."

"Huh? No. I'm from the South."

I look down and scratch my head. "Oh, weird. It's hard to hear, y' know?"

He nods but looks confused.

I go to the bar for a Red Bull and vodka.

"That's twelve dollars." She hands me a small plastic cupful.

"Twelve? Jesus." I flip through the cash I have left. I hadn't taken out too much so as not to go overboard. Being concerned with money goes against my life philosophy, but I still feel sick spending it, especially when it's cash and I'm seeing it fucking slip away, rather than just swiping a card.

"You wouldn't forget to tip your waitress now, would you?"

I sit down next to Ry and consider the futility of the concept of a strip club. Somehow it has convinced people to pay for sexual frustration. I think there is a simple and flawed logic at work here: proximity to a vagina is directly proportional to the odds of entering it. Clearly anyone could come up with a million scenarios in which this wouldn't be true. Maybe it's not even that complex. Maybe it's just: PUSSY.

I watch what must be a legal senior across from me. He has this intense, eyebrow-less perverse gaze that does not break for a moment.

"And even if you could do anything, you're in front of like all these people who you know are watching her, and you too. Can't really help that. Plus she obviously only gives a fuck about the money." I go on about it for a while, but after a while her breasts and the way her blond hair falls on them have me in a bit of a trance, and I can't help but imagine that if I put money down, maybe she would care about me or my body.

"I mean, it's not that bad, man. Kinda nice."

"Yeah, yeah, you're right." I feel a little foolish being so cynical. Gal is a few seats down, shelling money out like an ATM, hollering away and paying for the other guys' lap dances. I throw three dollars at her heels just before she walks off stage. The same seat across from me has now been filled by another old man who could've been his double.

I wish I had more guts. We're back at Gal's drinking more, and the guys are getting into some boxing on the porch. It's small and people keep getting knocked off into the bushes, into bystanders smoking butts. Someone with whom I'm vaguely acquainted sits next to me on the bench, and somehow we get into a heart to heart. Things are vague at this point from the booze.

"Can I tell you something, man? I haven't told anyone about this yet; I just found this out."

"Yeah, go ahead."

He looks at me with dark, sunken eyes. He's got a shaved head, and these stereotypical tattoos on his arms that probably don't mean too much.

"I just got diagnosed with CF today."

There's a long silence, and I want him to know how bad I feel, because I do feel it, but that kind of thing is never easy to say without sounding like a prerecorded message.

"But, you know, I don't want people to see me any differently. That's why I'm not gonna tell this to everyone. I want things to be the same right up 'til the end, you know? People start feeling bad and look at you differently and it's like, you can't just have a good time anymore. So I don't want that. That's bullshit, man. Not how I want to go out. Not how I want to die. And that's probably gonna happen soon, you know?"

His own words have worked himself into tears. "I just never thought that one minute I would have to go from this shit to thinking about my death. The fuckin' end man, the end. Out of nowhere. I just, never, could have imagined something like that. Do you know what that must be like?" His hands were shifting now, as if to make up for something that he couldn't express well enough in words.

"I can't imagine." I pause. "So why are you telling this to me, then? Because maybe you'll never see me again." I answer my own question. He nods and looks down.

We drink more beer and he starts boxing a shorter guy, stalky and fairly jacked. He is thrown down the steps in less than a minute. I open my throat, the rest of my beer funnels down, and I stand up, raising my arms in front of me.

"Put 'em on me." There's a few laughs. "Put the fuckin' gloves on me! Throw 'em on me!" In a moment I'm shuffled into the ring and tapping gloves. I'm not ready. My tap recoils into a block through which the first haymaker shatters. The second connects, right across my face. Left, right, left. I'm hit twice and spinning. Fuck me. I can't believe how much it throbs through my body and my head tingles, numb. There's dull pain, and my arms now shoot back up for the second tap and this time my body follows through. I'm all in and, in an instant, blowing sparks. I lean into the blows. His swings are too broad, the type of hit that comes from drunken pricks hopped up on testosterone, the kind that expects a lot and foresees little. They tilt him off his axis and leave him vulnerable during the recovery, though I don't know it at the time. I swing through the barrage, and the next thing I know he's fallen into some people and the ref says stop but I keep going, landing a solid hit on his side. It makes a satisfying sound, a muffled slap of glove against skin.

"Whoaaahh!"

I hear it all around me. I wipe my face and walk back to the starting point. Might've been a sucker punch, but it doesn't matter because in this moment I am alive, cleansed of all doubt and worry, right at the moment when I'm actually in danger. The next round starts. I fall off the steps onto my back. It kind of fizzles out now. I back off, sensing that I've crossed a precarious line. I have my little moment to take with me.

If only I had kept hitting. If only I had thrown the gloves off and dug my knuckles into his jaw and dyed his whiskers red. If only I had smacked his eye sockets shut and split his lip and made him a different man. If only I had faltered in the process, causing him to pin me down and ruin my face so that I could wake up the next day, blossoming in the mirror like a purple flower and knowing that I went all the way with something, that I had brought it home for once.

At the end of the night, Andy asks if I want to do something funny. Why not? We walk down to an old abandoned house at the edge of the woods. A lot has been cleared next to the cottage, hacked down from the woods but never built on, someone's vague ambition left out in the pale moonlight. We break in and trash it for fun. I hurt my foot trying to kick down the door, so after that I just watch him. Someone made the effort to lock the place even though it's barren inside. He shoves a lawnmower through a window and shatters the bathroom mirror. Broken shards crack under my feet. There are probably ghosts here and I'm growing tired. I go outside. I've had enough.

The stars are just as they were at the start, the only thing to retain any grace or tranquility out of this feverish night, but it was a night that I felt needed to happen nonetheless. This has been a man's night, and I will relish its emptiness.

Everyone needs some kind of release from the stress of leading lives that never once lived up to our childhood dreams, but underneath there was maybe something greater. I needed to know that the reason I never did this sort of thing wasn't because I was scared, wasn't because I wasn't "manly" enough. I think it's as simple as me not liking crowds.

I woke up the next day in beautiful agony, and all of the thoughts which would've normally been running through my head were absent. One percent of the world's population owns forty percent of planet's wealth, and fifty percent of the world lives on less than two dollars a day. Severe environmental damage worldwide is now irreversible, and there's no serious effort to stop it. Despite all this, I still woke up happy.

For once, instead of feeling detached, I felt real. If it weren't for nights like this, the weight of reality might be too heavy to bear.

At any rate, if I had gone home instead of getting in that truck, I don't think I would've been doing anything to help save the world.

Broken Ankles and Stern Talking-Tos: Why My Mom is the Best
Emily Murnane

My childhood best friend's name was Elinor Mileti, and I adored
her in every way. We hadn't always been friends, but I'd always
wanted to be her friend. She seemed absolutely flawless—she had
big, brown doe-eyes and was incredibly witty for a first-grader. And
her clothes were so cool. We all had to wear uniforms but had two
options for shoes and endless sock opportunities as long as they were
white, blue, or green. Her saddle shoes and white ankle socks were
so much better than my brown suede shoes and navy knee socks. My
friend Jillian and I spent a lot of time trying to get close to Elinor,
but she and her friends would make up ridiculous passwords that
we'd have to guess before we could hang out with them. We never
guessed them.

In second grade, both Elinor and I found that our best friends had
moved away and we had nobody to play with, so naturally we clung
to each other.

To say that I looked up to Elinor is an understatement. I idolized
her. I wanted my hair in a perfect messy bun like hers. I wanted to
read the same books she read. I wanted to have the same backpack
she had. When she started calling herself Elle and signing her name
with just the letter *L*, I started signing mine *M*. I wanted to be perfect and in my eyes, she was perfect. So I wanted to be just like her.

Elinor didn't seem to mind that I was being such a little copycat
because she was always at least one step ahead of me. She seemed
to get such joy out of reinventing herself anyway, and watching me
follow her was just extra entertainment.

After about a year of that, we settled into our own groove in which
we both got to be cool in our individual ways. Not that we were
popular, but Elinor was sure that I was cool enough to not totally
embarrass her, and I was sure that I was cool enough that she would

stay friends with me. And then, gradually or maybe all at once, we stopped worrying about how cool we were and relaxed into a normal friendship.

I spent a lot of time growing up at Elinor's house, and her family was very different from mine. Her parents were happily married but slept in separate bedrooms, which I found strange. She had a younger sister, which I did not. When I slept over at her house the first time, I almost starved to death because they didn't eat dinner until eight thirty, while my mom and I ate as soon as she got home around five. Elinor's mom made us play outside whether we wanted to or not, while my mom and I rented movies all the time. When I broke ankles at my house, I got comforted. When I broke ankles at the Miletis', Mrs. Mileti read me the riot act.

That's hyperbole, of course. I only broke one bone at Elinor's house, so I guess I don't really know if I would have gotten yelled at every time.

We were eight years old and it must have been autumn, because Elinor and I had spent most of the afternoon gathering all of the fallen leaves we could find on her parents' two acres of property. It was a leaf pile to be envied—three feet tall, quite wide, and with just enough crunch to be satisfying. We constructed the pile next to the stone wall that divided the Miletis' yard from their neighbors' so we could take turns jumping off the wall into our leaves. You see now where this is going.

Elinor took the first jump (she took the first everything), plunging into the leaves in a cannonball style that would have made her mother faint if she'd been looking out the window, which she wasn't. But we weren't stupid, and we'd taken care to be sure that our leaf pile was deep and wide enough to cushion our fall. Elinor rolled around in our handiwork for a minute, soaking it all in, I guess, and helped me rake and reshape it for my turn.

The stone wall was only three feet high. Elinor and I had spent days climbing and dropping out of trees twice as high, and nothing bad ever happened. But I jumped three feet into the leaf pile, cannonball-style just like my role model, and my right ankle snapped like a wishbone. I clamped my lips closed between my teeth for all of two seconds before I started bawling, and Elinor ran inside to get her mom.

Mrs. Mileti came running out the back door, and I rolled myself out of the leaves. I sobbed that my ankle was broken and she said something like, "Oh, it is not," and told me to follow her inside. So I hopped along after her on one foot.

She pulled out two chairs in the kitchen, one for me to sit on and another for me to prop my foot on. "You've just twisted it, that's all," she said, filling up a baggie with ice and cold water to put on it. Elinor sat quietly in a chair on the other side of the kitchen with eyes bulging in shock, hands folded in her lap.

This was not my first broken ankle. In fact, it was my third. The first one had happened at ballet class when I was six, and I turned my feet out into an extra-wide first position. The second break happened when I was eight, walking down the hallway at home. There had been dozens—no, hundreds—of other times when I'd just been standing somewhere and my ankle twisted for no goddamn reason and I suddenly found myself on the floor. I had weak ankles, but I always knew the difference between walk-it-off injuries and call-mom injuries.

Broken bones, to me, have always felt like a sort of non-pain. They hurt a bit, but you somehow know that you're not feeling as much of the pain as you should. Like if your hand was really cold and then you got a big gash in it, and you knew it was bad but you also knew you were sort of numb, so you keep waiting for it to get worse when your hand warms up. That, and nausea. That's how I knew it was broken, not twisted.

But it was pretty clear that Mrs. Mileti wasn't buying it.

"It's broken," I wailed. "I want my mommmm…"

"Would you just stop it?" Mrs. M. said. "You're fine." She rubbed her temples with her fingertips. To be fair, I don't think she was trying to be mean. She was a tough mom, and she was probably just trying to make me feel better by downplaying my injury. But that's not what I saw when I was eight. I feel like I spent most of my childhood trying to talk to grown-ups in terms they'd understand and eventually ending up in tears because they weren't taking me seriously. As a child who was experienced in the broken-ankle department, all I saw in that moment was yet another situation in which yet another adult didn't believe me when I clearly knew more than she did. My pain-tears turned to anger-tears and after several long minutes, Mrs. Mileti elected to call my mom after all.

My mom came and took me to the ER, and I spent the next two months on crutches. I'd break another ankle in a trampoline accident the next year, and the school nurse would accuse my mom of child abuse. Make no mistake: I wasn't abused. I was perfectly capable of getting hurt on my own, and I'd make it an art as a teenager.

I realized then, the day of broken ankle number three, exactly how lucky I was to have my mom instead of somebody else's. It seems like such a silly revelation to have over a broken ankle, but I realized even at eight years old that my mom and dad were unlike other adults because they treated me like a person instead of like a kid. If I'd told my mom my ankle was broken, she wouldn't have questioned it. She'd have trusted me. If I'd had another mom, I might have been tougher but as it was, I was happier.

Salem Street, Lowell

Pat Willwerth

"This is it, Willsa, this is it," said Mark, slapping me on the back and tapping his foot like an RLS poster boy. We were two nineteen-year-old kids with our first apartment. "Patty boy, this is it!"

We were on our back porch, sitting on our asses because we didn't have any furniture yet. The porch hung at about a thirty-degree angle to the ground.

"Holy shit," my dad said earlier that afternoon as we lugged an old washing machine up the wobbly wooden steps leading up three stories to the porch. "Don't let anybody out on this porch, for God's sakes. This thing looks like it's going to collapse any minute. I've heard enough stories about people partying on their porches, then the goddamned thing collapses. People get killed that way. Be smart, will ya?"

I can't be sure exactly, because I didn't count, but I'd say the largest number of people we ever had out there was around twenty-five. We had one friend who refused to set foot on the porch. He had to hang his head out my bedroom window to smoke with us.

We were on the third floor, and there was an identical porch below us. A Brazilian woman and her white boyfriend owned that porch. The guy was young, tall, and muscular, with tattoos and a bad case of the crazy eye. She was older, fatter, and always had a pack of generic brand cigarettes, whatever was cheapest at the Spanish convenience store down the street, stuck between her exposed bra and giant, sagging, brown breasts. If you walked in the back door from their porch, you'd get to the kitchen. That was where they cooked crack and made meth. They would come upstairs sometimes to sell us painkillers, stolen DVDs that they wheeled around in a shopping cart, and once I bought a guitar from them, worth at least $100, for $5.

There was another porch below that one, which was tilted at the same angle, but was attached to the ground. If you walked in that back door, you'd get to the kitchen of a single mother from somewhere in South America who didn't speak much English. She lived with her two sons and two daughters, all under the age of eight.

Behind the porches and enclosed by a wooden fence was a cement lot that, despite the South American woman constantly sweeping it, seemed always to be covered in shattered glass. Standing in the middle of the lot was a small, single-family house that no one lived in, and the top of its chimney was about eye level if you stood on our porch. The chimney was a good twenty feet away, so we tried to flick our cigarette butts into it, which was pretty damn hard. About ten of them made it in. We probably tried three hundred times, at least. When the South American mother and her four kids moved from the first floor apartment to that house, she probably found ten cigarette butts at the bottom of her new fireplace, and hundreds more at her doorstep.

To our left and over a small wooden picket fence was a cement lot exactly like ours, with two apartment buildings. The apartment buildings each had three back porches, angled just like ours.

That first day, I heard a lot of screaming coming from the third floor apartment facing me from the next lot over. A tall, young Brazilian man climbed out of the window onto his porch.

"What's up, man?" I yelled.

"Nothing, man," he said, hyperventilating, eyes and head darting around like a sparrow. "My girl, man, she's having a baby, man. I'm going to the hospital. Yo, I'll stop by later."

That was the first time we met Davi. He became our friend, used to come over when he got in a fight with his girlfriend, which happened at least three times a week, and he'd drink liquor and give us shots of whatever he was drinking. Sometimes he would punch the wooden support beams on our porch and say, "At least it's not her, man." We let him and his buddy cook crack in our kitchen a few times. Burnt the shit out of half our spoons.

That first night, Mark and I spent the last hours of sunlight lighting candles all through the apartment. We needed the candles because we didn't have electricity yet. No refrigerator either, so we had a cooler in every room filled with Keystone Light and PBR.

We were two suburban white boys, me and Mark, me more so than him. It was our first night in our place, our own place, and we were going to have a goddamn party. We invited all of our white-boy and white-girl suburban friends over, lit the candles, and ravaged the coolers. We sat cross-legged on the floor playing Asshole and Whist by flickering candlelight. No furniture, no lights, no stereo, but we had our floor, our candles and coolers, and we sang loud enough that even if there had been a stereo, it would have been overpowered by our slurred voices.

That was enough for us. Anything to be out of our white suburban parents' houses, anything to be out of the dorms. Not that I was allowed to live in the dorms anymore anyway. If I set foot in a residential building for the next seven months, so I was told by campus police, I would be arrested for trespassing.

About 11:00 PM, I ran out of cigarettes, so I decided to take a walk down my new street, hoping to find a convenience store that would still be open, holding my head high, whistling to my drunk self and looking around at my new neighborhood. The side of the street opposite me was lined the whole way down with little brick projects, three rows of them, extending all the way back to the street parallel mine.

I was walking on my side of the street when I saw a big black man closing the metal gate to a driveway alongside a three family building. He stopped for a second, looked me up and down, and said in a deep voice, "You don't look like you belong here."

I looked up and smiled timidly. "What?" I kind of muttered.

"You don't *look* like you be*long* here," he said slowly. He didn't smile.

Everyone seemed to be staring at me as I walked by. Groups of people—blacks, Hispanics, Cambodians—were sitting on just about every stoop, and they stopped talking and stared when I walked by. Not everyone on the stoops across the street at the projects noticed me, but those who did stopped talking and stared at me, too. I got to the store after walking about five minutes, bought a pack of Marlboros, pulled my hoodie all the way over my head to conceal my pasty white face, and started walking home with my head down, staring at the cracked pavement.

I was a little more than halfway home when I heard someone mutter, "Hey, man."

I kept walking without acknowledging the voice, and then it yelled, "Yo, buddy."

I turned around and walked back. "What's up?" I asked in a prepubescent squeak.

"You got a cigarette?"

"Yeah. I just got 'em, though. Gotta pack 'em first." I slapped the new pack of butts against my palm three times, flipped it around, slapped it another three times, and gave the man a cigarette.

He nodded at me and lit up.

That was the way I would walk to and from that store: head down, hoodie stretched over my forehead, walking fast, but not so fast that I would attract any attention.

I got over that after a few months. Nothing happened in particular to make me feel this way, but I just didn't feel like I had to anymore, and I didn't. I was friends with Davi. He claimed to be a member of the Bloods, and he said that he'd take care of me if anyone gave me any shit. I don't know that he actually would have. I would imagine that if another Blood, or an MS-13, had bashed my head against a curb, there wouldn't be much he could have done about it, and though we were pretty good friends, I was an outsider.

He lived with his white American girlfriend, their baby daughter, his girlfriend's white American mother, the mother's white American boyfriend, and Davi's Brazilian uncle. I used to go over there once or twice a week for dinner. We had four or five kids constantly sleeping on our floor at this point, and I was the only one who ever really went over to Davi's, but his girlfriend would send me back with food for everyone.

So I never had a problem with any of the neighbors, but some of my friends weren't as lucky as me, or maybe they just weren't as smart. Julian definitely just wasn't as smart. Julian was even more of a white boy than me, from a suburb of Boston near my suburban hometown, but a richer suburb with more trees and fewer blacks, Hispanics, and maybe the same number of Asians. Julian left our apartment one night after a few beers and some smoke. He disappeared for a minute or two, then came bursting through the back door. Blood was gushing from his nose, and his left eye was already black and blue.

"What the fuck happened to you?" asked Mark.

"Dude," said Julian, stammering his words and clutching his swollen face, "I'm walking outside, right? And some big Spanish dude comes up to me, right in front of your fuckin' driveway, and asks me, 'What are you doing in my neighborhood?' and I'm like, 'Your neighborhood,' and he fuckin' punches me in the fuckin' face."

"Well, Jules," said Mark, with a smile stretching across his face, "you're a fucking moron, and you deserved that."

Julian did deserve that. Mark and I learned early and often that the apartment was our apartment, the porch was our porch, but the neighborhood would never be ours. We walked the streets without much fear, we talked with the neighbors, we carved our names into the wet cement of the sidewalk they laid down one afternoon, but the neighborhood never was, and never could be ours, not like when we were growing up. For the first time in our lives, we were a minority.

We weren't the only whites on the street, but we were pretty damn close. The store where I bought my cigarettes was filled with mostly Spanish food items that I had never heard of. I can't even remember the name of the store because it was a Spanish surname that was hard to pronounce. Standing on our back porch you'd hear the same Spanish reggaeton rhythm pouring out of six different windows, that, *"umm—chuck-mm-chuck—umm—chuck-mm-chuck,"* over and over, like a skipping record, all day and all night. Sometimes I would hear Guns N' Roses, but that was just because they used to blast GNR at Davi's house a lot. La Negra Pop was the name of the local record shop. I didn't recognize a single goddamn artist they sold. They sold do-rags there too, a whole section full of them, some with visors, and some without.

We got robbed once, at gunpoint. Twice, actually. The first time it happened, it was a sunny day outside, kind of cold, but I was in an especially good mood anyway. I was in the shower singing Beatles songs, and I didn't stop singing when I got out to towel myself off. I didn't stop when I wrapped the towel around my waist and danced into the living room to grab my beer.

"Gooood day sunnshine," I sang, trailing off as I noticed the pale faces of my friends sitting on the empty kegs we used as chairs. Mark had his face in his hands and was clawing through his dark hair. "You guys alright?" I asked.

No one said anything for a second, then Mark looked up and smiled. "Willsa, we just got robbed."

"What do you mean?" I asked. "Did you see the guy? What'd they take?"

"Willsa," said Mark, his smile growing bigger. "He had a gun. He robbed us at gunpoint. Took all the yay, all the weed, all the cash, all the rolls—Willsa, we got robbed, buddy."

It turned out to be a BB gun, and one of our friends went and found the guy and got everything back for us. The next time it was a real gun. I forgot to mention this earlier, but Mark sold a shit-load of weed, coke, ecstasy, Xanax, and whatever else he could get his hands on. Eventually, he would get arrested for trafficking cocaine across a state border, but at this point he was doing one hell of a business. The money was good, but there was not a person on that block who didn't know that our apartment had a shit-load of drugs and money in it. I don't blame people for trying to get in there. We were two white-boy dragons sleeping in front of one hell of a treasure. The second time the apartment got robbed, I was in Boston. It was a real gun that time, a pistol, and they held the tip of the barrel against Mark's head. Mark wasn't stupid, but he was cocky, and he was selling too many drugs, showing it off at too many parties, and leaving the front door unlocked.

I eventually moved out of that place. The drugs were getting to be too much, and after Mark got busted, an undercover cop parked in front of our house twenty-four hours a day. We got raided twice. I sublet the place to a couple who had a lot of the same friends as Mark and I did. On the last night of their lease, someone was shot to death in the kitchen during a party. Two people got in an argument over a game of beer pong, and one of them shot the other one. To death. They were each in a different gang. The one who got shot had just gotten out of jail, sentenced for raping a thirteen year old when he was sixteen, or something like that. I think he was eighteen when he got shot.

I never had any problems, though. Close, I guess, but nothing. In fact, I saw a lot of beauty while I was living there. I loved standing on the back porch, leaning over the railing and staring across the cement lots at the tall, brick smokestack rising from the old abandoned mill alongside the Merrimack River. Around the holiday season, they put green Christmas lights around the smokestack to make it look like a Christmas tree, complete with a big shining star on top. About halfway between my deck and the smokestack was a big cement high rise dorm, and when it rained you could watch the water soak the cement, staining it dark, starting at the top, and slowly crawling its way to the ground.

My view was saturated with the tops of roofs, all different colors, and tall, pointy church steeples. The city was dirty and poor. A washed-up mill town, sucked dry and spit into the winds of time, left in the dust the Industrial Revolution kicked up behind its screeching tires. The city was beautiful, though, like a girl who fell off her bike when she was four and smashed her face against the pavement. Her teeth never grew in straight, and the scars never fully healed, but she grew up with so much pride and dignity that though the boys teased her, they admired her nonetheless.

They loved her.

I loved her dive pubs and liquor stores with black metal bars over the windows, her gas stations with bulletproof glass windows that you weren't allowed to enter. You put your money in a slot and the teller passed a pack of Marlboro reds through the same slot, conversing through a microphone. I loved her screaming police sirens—the Lowell alarm clock, we called them. I loved her clotheslines, draped across wooden support beams on dripping porches, her tents by the banks of the river where a community of homeless men and women built trash-can fires and drank forties. I loved and admired her hideous beauty, and one day, something beautiful happened to me on that back porch.

I was sitting in my room playing my guitar, playing very quietly because I wasn't, and I still am not, all that good. I was trying to block out the clumsy round of *umm—chuck-mm-chuck* floating softly through my window, when all of a sudden, the sound was obliterated by some chords from a single acoustic guitar. The guitar was singing three chords, and the tune sounded familiar, though I couldn't quite put my finger on what it was. I took a second to learn the chords, then I climbed out my window to the back porch, pulling my guitar through behind me. An old Brazilian man was sitting on the porch below Davi's, cigar hanging from his mouth, playing an old beat-up six-string. I started playing along with him and he looked over, nodded his head and yelled something I didn't understand.

I nodded back, and suddenly he started singing in Portuguese. I didn't understand a word of what he said, but I recognized the tune. It was "Knockin' on Heaven's Door." When he hit the chorus, it sounded something like, "Donyay donyay donyay da la port day cell," and when the chorus ended, he stopped singing, but kept playing and stared at me. I started singing, "I can't shoot them anymore," as he smiled and kept strumming. When it got back to the chorus, we both started singing a little louder. He sang, "Donyay donyay donyay da la port day cell," and I sang, "knock knock knockin' on Heaven's door," and I think we sounded alright, not like two drunks trying to sing the same song while each one slurs the wrong verse. A few of the neighbors seemed to like it, at least. They came out their back doors or stuck their heads out their windows, staring at thisold, weather beaten, dark-skinned Brazilian man and this tall, pale, white kid with a patchy beard singing Dylan together in two different languages.

When we ran out of verses, we took turns laying the chords down and soloing, and when that fizzled out, the old man signaled with his index finger for me to come over.

"You want me to come over?" I yelled to him. He acted like he hadn't heard a word, and kept signaling with his old, brown finger. I ran down the steps with my guitar in my hand, ran over the shattered glass and cigarette butts, through the lot to the street, down his driveway, up his stairs, and sat down on the floor of his wooden deck.

"What's up, man?" I asked.

He said nothing, just laughed, exposing the few teeth he had left, all of which were stained like they had a coat of yellow shellac over them.

"Nice playing, man. What else do you know?" I asked.

Again he just laughed, then he started strumming his guitar. He didn't speak a lick of English.

His friend, another Brazilian man who appeared to be about the same age, with the same wood-polished teeth and weather-beaten brown skin, who also spoke no English, walked outside onto the deck and handed me a burning joint. We finished smoking, and the two of them sang some old folk songs that they knew in Portuguese, while one of them strummed chords on the guitar, and I soloed quietly below it all. Eventually an old woman, who I assume was one of their wives, came outside and gave us each a plate of rice, pinto beans and tender pork with a lot of hot spices on it. I said thank you, but she just smiled with her yellow teeth and laughed, muttering something in Portuguese.

After an hour or so of listening to these old Brazilian folk tunes, I noticed that some of my friends were starting to congregate on my porch for the night's party. They looked at me like I was nuts for a second, then started laughing and called me over. I said good-bye to the old men and headed back to my place, where I answered questions about what the hell I was doing over there.

"They don't speak English?"

"Nah."

"So how the hell did you talk to them? They gave you dinner too?"

We couldn't talk, but we spoke about Dylan and guns and heaven. We spoke about G major chords, old Brazil, and the suburbs. We spoke about the smokestack, the Merrimack, and the way the raindrops soak that old cement high-rise.

Baku, Azerbaijan

Agata Ayrapetova

i.

The corners of the black and white photograph are bent or torn off. It is stained in many places and ripped on the side. The condition of the photograph and the image portrayed in it suggest that it was taken long ago and handled many times.

It is a picture of my family—the only photograph we have of us together. It was taken at my grandmother's house in Baku, the capital of Azerbaijan. My father is just thirty-one and my mother is twenty-seven. Both look a lot older in the photograph than their actual age. My father's face is oddly striking. He seems as though he is trying to keep a straight face, smiling but with his mouth closed. There is a sparkle in his eyes. I can't decide whether he is happy or sad. Is he trying to keep from smiling or crying? In the moment, he looks happy. My father's arms are around my older sister and my baby brother. On his left thigh sits my six-year-old sister with her hand gripping on to my father's watch. My baby brother, who is about two years old, is sitting on his right thigh, looking away into space. My father's left hand is firmly supporting my sister and his right hand is resting on my brother's legs. My mother is sitting on the right side of my father. It's the dark circles under her eyes that make her look older. The smile on her face seems sincere yet weak.

She knows something we don't. As always, my mother is wearing her gold hoop earrings. One day when I am old enough, she says, she'll give them to me. I am sitting on my mother's lap, looking straight into the camera with my mouth slightly open. I am three years old. I am a child who is completely oblivious to the surreal dynamic of the family and unaware of how soon it will end.

On the back of the photograph, in green ink, is inscribed in

Russian the date the photograph was taken: "1982 god, Mai" (year 1982, May). There is something else written in cursive handwriting that is boldly crossed out with a blue pen. The only visible word is Serioshka, my mother's affectionate name for my father Sergei. My mother wrote both the date and what looks like couple of crossed out sentences about my father.

"Looking at the photographs again?" my mother asked recently with a smile as she saw me sitting on the floor with photo albums and boxes of family photographs all around me. As I inspected the photograph carefully, she looked over my shoulder. After a moment of silence and hesitation she spoke.

"Soon after this photograph was taken, your father went away for a while," she said, sighing. In all my twenty-one years, she had never spoken of this. "He left me all alone with three children to take care of." I felt uncomfortable. A part of me wanted her to stop, yet another part wanted to know more. She said no more.

ii.

I was born on September 4, 1979 in Baku. My sister Artemis, who is three years older than me, and my parents' first child, told me in her smug way that I was an accident. "You're not even supposed to be here. You know that? Nobody was excited when you were born." My mother says I was an unexpected child, a surprise.

When my mother realized that she was pregnant with me, she was convinced I was a boy. She picked out a couple of names for me: Edward and Agat. Edward was a name her father wanted to name his son. Unfortunately, he had six daughters. My mother was the middle child. She was certain that her father disliked her, mainly for her stubbornness, because she was constantly punished—insulted, yelled at, and beaten. According to him, she was to blame for all that went wrong. She laughed at him.

My mother was the only daughter who went on to college, and

consequently became the favored daughter. Her parents took her out shopping and bought her black leather knee high boots as a token of their appreciation. She soon became a schoolteacher. She taught art, drafting in particular, to grades six to ten. With the pregnancy of her first child, my mother left her job to become a full-time mom. She loved being a teacher, but being a mother was much more important to her and my father.

Agat was a name my mother discovered while reading a Greek novel. It was a name of a young Greek gentleman who was as handsome as he was clever and brave. The name Agat became a representation of this impressionable Greek hero.

When my mother gave birth to a pale, seven-pound baby girl, she was bewildered and wasn't sure what to name me, so in need of a name at the last minute she added a letter "a" to the ending of Agat and made it my name. While this was taking place, my father nervously paced outside of the delivery room window with flowers and champagne to celebrate the birth of his baby boy.

This reminds me of an Armenian joke I once heard. A man is waiting outside the hospital for the arrival of his child while his wife is in labor inside the hospital. A nurse runs outside to let the father know that the wife just gave birth.

"Is it a boy?" the man yells.

"No," the nurse replies.

Astonished, the man asks, "What is it, then?"

My mother says I was a quiet child and didn't require as much attention as Artemis.

"Even when you were born, it was as though you weren't here," my sister teased me. "I got all the attention. Always."

Long ago, during Christmas time, Artemis picked a shiny glass Christmas ornament off our Christmas tree and bit into it. Blood gushed from as sharp pieces of the ornament stuck out of her little mouth. My mother panicked, not so much for my sister's well-being, but in fear of my father's reaction.

There was another incident when my sister's playmate pushed her off a second-floor balcony. She fell to the ground head first, splitting her forehead open. Blood covered her whole face, dripping into her mouth, getting all over her clothes.

Things like that never happened to me. I have never mistaken a Christmas ornament for a fruit, and I was always too scared to play on the second floor, especially near the ledge.

When I was about six years old, I became very sick. My mother did not take me to the hospital at first. She took care of me at home. For days I slept on our kitchen couch fully clothed, under several blankets, drinking sweet tea with lemon and honey. One night things became worse. I groaned, screamed, and cried in my sleep, out of weakness and pain. I opened my eyes when I sensed a bright light in the room and someone's presence. My mother stood in front of the open refrigerator. She soaked a towel in cold vodka and tied it around my neck to bring my body temperature down. The wetness and odor of the cloth around my neck caused more discomfort, as I lay in the dark with my eyes closed, half unconscious. The next time I awoke was to a cold hand on my sweaty forehead.

As I opened my tired eyes, I noticed a pale young nurse with a stethoscope sitting on the couch in front of me. In her nightgown, my mother stood next to me. I wanted to know what was going on, but I couldn't make a sound. I was too weak. The stethoscope felt very cold on my chest.

"Slowly breathe in...breathe out," said the nurse. "Good girl."

I was taken to the hospital the next day. I had hepatitis and it wasn't safe for my family and me to stay at home. The hospital smelled like medicine and sick people. My mother held on to my hand as I clutched her. The nurses looked big and mean and not at all gentle like the one at home. I couldn't hold back my tears.

"Mama, I want to go home," I cried.

"You have to stay here. You are very sick and I am not able to take proper care of you anymore. The doctors have to take care of you now. Soon when you feel better, I will come and take you home. Until then you have to stay here and let these people take care of you. Do what they say," my mother explained.

I was stricken with fear when I realized she was soon leaving me here, all alone. My mother was not staying with me in the hospital like she did with my baby brother when he was sick. Why? Was I not her child? Did she not love me enough to stay with me? I let her go without saying anything because she already knew what I was feeling. I did not cry when I saw her walking out the door. I cried hysterically when I could no longer see her. She was gone and I was alone for the first time in my life at six years old.

The hospital was filled with people. There seemed to be no available rooms. The nurse told me to follow her around the hospital for available spaces. All beds were already occupied. We ended up in the hallway from where we started, near a dirty couch outside the hospital rooms. People sat on this dark couch while they waited either to see their loved ones, or just for the sake of it. The nurse told me that this couch was now my bed and I was to stay on this couch at all times, unless told otherwise.

I sat down and looked out at the doors from which my mother disappeared. I buried my face in the dirty cushion and cried. My little fingers felt holes in the cushions. Soon the nurse brought me two huge orange pills and a cup of water.

"Take them and go to sleep," she said as she walked away. I tried swallowing the first one, but it would not go down my throat. It was too big and it smelled. I gagged on the pill and threw up on the couch. There was nobody to clean it up. I stuck the orange pills in the couch holes I discovered earlier and went to sleep around my vomit.

The same nurse woke me up for breakfast in the morning. I had no sense of what time it was. My vomit was already embedded into the couch. The nurse didn't notice anything, and I was glad. She was a big woman with a thick black braid and a little black mustache.

There were moles all over her face, some with hairs sticking out of them. Her arms were thick and hairy. Her fingers were short and chunky. She gave me her massive hand and I grabbed on to her finger. Her whole hand was too big to grasp. She dragged me to a table. There was a bowl of brown kasha—overcooked clumps of cereal—and two orange pills on a table.

"Eat. When the bowl is empty, you can go back to the couch."

I couldn't eat. I stared into space and the sick people all around me. I felt thirsty, but there was no water on the table. I took my spoon and placed it in the bowl of kasha, and swirled it around. The kasha reminded me of my vomit from last night. I took the monster pills in my hand and walked back to the abandoned couch. Once again I stuck the pills in the holes of the cushion and started crying, looking out the doors that led to the outside. I was thirsty and lonely. All the children in the hospital seemed to have their moms or dads staying with them, except me.

At the time I was sick, my father was away. Where he was I don't know—away on business, I guess. Because my father was away for so long, he was partially erased from my mind and memories, as though he didn't really exist.

Looking back, I realize that my mother, who had three children to support all on her own, couldn't afford to stay with me in the hospital. She worked when she could, usually during the day when we were at school. Once my mother came to the hospital during visiting hours, the only time she was allowed to see me. The visiting hours took place in a huge room. A huge plastic window divided the room, for safety reasons, mostly to protect the transmission of illnesses. On one side of the room stood a huge crowd of mostly families, and on the other patients eager to see their visitors. I was led into this tightly packed room and told that my mother was there to see me. As I entered the crowd, I felt invisible. I looked down at the people's feet as I began my journey through the crowd. When I looked up, I saw the plastic divider. I stood on my toes to look beyond people's heads, faces, and voices. In the distance, through the wide stained window that separated my mother from me, I saw my mother's face among many foreign faces. She was yelling out my name while reaching her arms out to me. This was as close as I got to my mother.

While I was in the hospital, my long, black, wavy hair became infested with lice. Once again the nurse escorted me into the bathroom, where she sloppily and carelessly chopped off chunks of hair. She expressed no sympathy, only disgust, as she vigorously pulled on my hair. After she was done with me, my hair was very short and unevenly spiky. I felt violated and naked coming out of the urine-tainted bathroom. I felt exposed. I had no way of hiding my naked head.

The next day the same dark nurse appeared in the distance with someone small trailing behind her, obscured by the nurse's massive body. A shock of pure joy shot down my spine when I caught a glimpse of my grandmother's wrinkled, sympathetic face. Tears filled my eyes and ran uncontrollably down my swollen face. My grandmother was the only person in front of whom I could cry. She never thought me weak for crying. She never criticized me. She loved me because I reminded her a lot of herself, or she says.

"Agata…Agata…Don't cry. I'm here to be with you. You are still my beautiful angel," she said as she held me tight to her bosom. "I have something for you from your mother." She reached into her purse and pulled out a beautifully embroidered cotton scarf to cover my bald head. It was blue and white and it smelled like my mother, my home. My grandmother tied it around my small head, hiding part of my discomfort.

"Agata, don't sit by the doors anymore. It's going to make you sicker. Stay on the couch. Okay?" my grandmother said before she left me.

I adored my new scarf. It became my security. That night as I went to bed, I stuffed it under my head instead of wearing it. It was safer that way. The next morning it was gone. Once again my head was exposed, and my mother seemed far away, like a fantasy, a dream. I cried frantically for my mother while looking for my heavenly scarf.

I looked for it everywhere. I stopped searching when I saw my nurse. I despised her, not because she was witch-like—mean and ugly—but because she was wearing my precious scarf.

After a month of treatment, which included a special diet and doses of harsh medication, I was allowed to go home. Apparently I was cured. My mother picked me up from the hospital. The day was gray, but my mother didn't care. She took me to the movie theater and bought me ice cream. As we slowly walked down the street, I held on to my mother's hand. I was the happiest girl in the world, even though I was bald. At home, my sister and brother were overflowing with questions.

"You were in the hospital for a long time," my baby brother said.

"Yeah, like three years," I replied.

iii.

Looking back at childhood times, I recognize my father as a hero, as well as a source of lost childhood memories. He was frequently away. I knew nothing of my father's whereabouts, except my mother's persuasive explanation that he was away on business.

Often, with the return of my father from what seemed like a never-ending "business trip," came happiness and excitement along with misery, anguish, and pain. He often brought us presents to make up for the times he wasn't there. Seeing him reminded me of how tall and handsome he really was. I felt very proud to have him as my father. He looked happy. His shiny black hair looked a lot longer than the last time I saw him. He embraced me and I clutched his neck. He smelled like body odor and cigarettes. I didn't want to let go.

Whenever my father was present, he was angry and never satisfied. It was very easy to make him angry, especially for a young child. I was never good enough for him. "Can't you do anything?" was a question my father often asked me. It is possible that through his criticism, he secretly expressed his love for me, but it was hard to tell since his criticism came with aggressive and cruel shouting.

As a child, I found my father strong, protective, mean, and unpredictable. I loved him and I hated him. I was proud of him, yet at times I wished he would disappear and never come back. My mother, on the other hand, feared this more than anything in the world.

"It's not his fault," my mother would say, so often that it got entrenched into my brain. "He had a rough childhood. His own mother placed him in an orphanage. He might seem mean to you, but he's a good father and a great man. Be grateful. If it wasn't for him you wouldn't have all that you have today. You wouldn't even be here." She never did mention how he was as a husband.

My parents met while my mother was teaching. At the time, my father owned a business shop in the neighborhood where she lived. After two months of dating each other, they got married. Before they even met my father served in the Soviet Army, in the Far East, in Vladivostok and Kamchatka peninsula. I asked my father why he never talked about it.

"It's not important," he replied. "You have to understand the communist system is extremely corrupt. I lost my best friend in the army. To speak of what went on in Vladivostok and Kamchatka is or used to be unthinkable and extremely dangerous, and now it's just unthinkable."

I sensed his uneasiness about the subject in his serious attempt to conceal what went on in Vladivostok and Kamchatka by dismissing it.

I learned of my father's childhood from my grandmother. She was very open about telling me everything.

"When I got pregnant with your father, I wanted to have an abortion. I didn't want him." Hearing this gave me the chills. "When he was born, I immediately wanted to give him away, because I knew he would be just like his father."

At times I thought that the mere presence of my mother, my siblings, and me made my father angry. His short temper was often reflected in his strict and unmerciful physical discipline over us—the rest of the family. I was never warned—I was immediately punished. A spanking was a treat coming from him.

My father kept his stereo on the kitchen counter. It was his, which meant it was absolutely off limits to us. I don't know what was going through my mind as I kept pressing on the stereo buttons until one of the buttons broke. What was I thinking? A feeling of complete terror came over me as I stood in front of my father's broken stereo. I quickly tried thinking of all the ways I could possibly get away with this. There was no way except going to sleep and hoping never to wake up again. I was too nervous to sleep, so in bed I waited for my father's arrival.

"Who touched my stereo?" Oh God. I was terrified. "Agata!" yelled out my father from the kitchen.

I got out of bed, shaking uncontrollably as I walked out into the kitchen. My baby brother heard the tone of my father's voice and poked his head into the kitchen.

"Did you break the button on the stereo?" my father loudly asked me while looking straight into my eyes, already knowing the answer. Veins were popping out of his forehead. He knew I did it because he could see the fear in me. I heard my brother pacing in another room.

"I didn't do it," I said very unconvincingly, on the verge of tears. I was never a good liar.

"Did you break the button on the stereo?" he yelled, gradually approaching me, like a wild animal toward a prey, ready to strike.

"I—" While on the verge of confessing, I suddenly got interrupted by my baby brother, who was now in the same room.

"I did it," he said without any hesitation. "I broke it." This was completely unexpected for both my father and me. My brother, who is a year and a half younger than I am, had never stood up for me before.

He was the fourth and the last child born to my mother. Born premature and sickly, he was kept in the hospital and my mother stayed with him, at all times. He was her little angel. My mother would not let him out of her sight. In kindergarten, pre-school, and school, my mother arranged that my brother and I would be in the same building, in case he needed anything.

"Watch him at all times," my mother said to me every morning before school. And I did. I was there for him no matter how inconvenient it was for me.

iv.

Usually on my way to school early in the morning, I stopped by my friend Natasha's house to see if she wanted to walk with me. My mother never approved of this. I had to knock several times before Natasha appeared at the door. A smell of cigarettes and alcohol escaped from the house with the opening of the screeching door. Inside, a pile of crumpled newspapers, clothes, and vodka bottles were scattered over the light brown linoleum floor. Natasha was a Russian girl with pale white skin, blue eyes and short, light blonde hair. She was my best friend at school, even though we did not sit next to each other in class. I sat in the back of the classroom with a boy by the name of Nikolai, who constantly picked his potato-shaped nose and smeared the results under the table. One day in November 1988, at the end of the school day, my teacher, Elvira Vartanovna, asked to see me. As she waited for the classroom to empty, she called me over to her.

"It would be in your parents' best interest to stop sending you to this school," she calmly said. "As an Armenian, it is no longer safe for you to be here. Tomorrow I do not want to see you in this school."

I had never stood this close to her before. For the first time in three years, I noticed her thick black eyelashes covered with even blacker mascara, and her heavy eyebrows that were very close to being connected in the middle. Her thin red-colored lips looked brighter than usual. Her face was rough and not at all feminine. I was so engaged in analyzing her face that I couldn't really focus on what she was telling me, until she said, "Tell your parents."

She then said again what she said earlier: "Stop coming to school."

My parents were not at all surprised when I told them about what had happened in school that day. They dismissed it right away, as though it had never happened. After a week of not going to school, during my family's last days in the country of Azerbaijan, at nine years old, I became more aware that war was breaking out between Azerbaijan and Armenia, over a piece of an ancient disputed territory, called Nagorno-Karabakh. Armenians in Azerbaijan were under constant threat. This was the reason for being deprived of my education and constantly having to deny my true nationality. This was the reason for leaving behind nine years of my life and everything that came with it. This was also the reason for thousands of innocent deaths. This was the beginning of the war between Azerbaijan and Armenia that is still taking place today.

Less than a week later, while my sister, brother, and I were asleep, my father, with the help of my mother, rearranged the furniture in the house to prevent anyone from entering. I woke up to the sound of a heavy piece of furniture being dragged against the wooden floors, scratching it deeply. In bed with my siblings, half awake, I listened carefully to the voices of the people moving the furniture. I was awake now, but pretending to be asleep. My mom spoke as quietly as humanly possible yet I could still detect fear in her voice. My father's words were expressed in a way that revealed signs of anger that soon enough would viciously appear. I wanted to go back to sleep, but I couldn't. My stomach felt weak; I felt nervous, scared. My body felt numb, inert, yet my mind was fully awake, aware, racing, trying to make sense of what was going on.

"Pick it up!" my father half yelled while trying to maintain his temper and sanity.

"I'm trying...keep your voice down," said my mother in a trembling voice. "The kids are asleep...."

"Pick it up or leave it. You're making this more difficult," said my father loudly, a bubble of violence bursting into his throat.

"Keep your voice down..." my mother replied calmly, yet fearfully. "The kids...."

I buried my face in the hard mattress, covering my ears with the thick wool blanket. I couldn't silence their voices, so I cried without making a sound. I felt better when I became convinced that my sister and my baby brother were deeply asleep. At least they were not able to hear this.

Our only door was double locked. Heavy furniture was placed in front of the kitchen door in case someone broke through the locks. The wooden blackout window shades were tightly shut, hiding any evidence of life inside. Through the cracks of the wooden blackout windows came our only source of light. Several suitcases, filled with necessary items, leaned against one another on the kitchen floor beside the couch where my parents often took their love naps. During these love naps was the only time I saw my parents showing affection towards each other. There were still a lot of unpacked household items that almost begged to be packed up and taken with us. Our shiny furniture that once seemed extremely large to me looked smaller than ever. Most of our clothing, books, photographs, and other household personal items still remained in their places. My father made it very clear to us to pack only what we could carry. He promised that when things settled down he would come back to Baku and get the rest of our belongings.

The next day, at five o'clock in the morning, we were waiting quietly, patiently in our house, which was in darkness, for the opportunity to run. Armed Azeri soldiers stood outside our barred bedroom windows. In the middle of the rowdy street stood tanks one after another, in a row. My father, replacing panic with anger, commanded us to stay away from the windows. My mother, who looked paler than usual, was not able to speak. She sat on the bed my siblings and I once slept on, rocking back and forth, mumbling some sort of a prayer. Seeing her like this seemed to intensify the harsh existing condition, making everything seem so much worse. I wanted to scream and cry, but I couldn't in front of my family. I held back my tears. Crying did nothing but express weakness, at least according to my father.

An ancient Soviet taxi drove us to the airport before sunrise. The airport was filled with Armenian families fleeing to Armenia, just as we were. Children were crying. People were pushing each other while rushing in the same direction—toward the plane. While standing in the ticket line, a tall man in black, whose face I success-fully erased from my memory, called my father a jerk because my father would not let him cut into the line in front of us. My father looked tired and very angry. Knowing my father and his very limited temper, I suddenly felt numb. Trying to keep my father from a full-on fist fight in front of everybody, including his children, my mother fainted. On the plane, the flight attendants, in dark blue suits with a gold pin over their chest, stood in a circle at a distance, talking and pointing at my father.

Less than a year later my father went back to Azerbaijan, with a fake passport and a different name. On his arrival in Baku, he went directly to our deserted house. Our kitchen door was knocked down, our windows were broken, our furniture destroyed, clothing stolen and family photographs smeared with feces on the bathroom floor. He left with nothing but agony.

CPSIA information can be obtained at www.ICGtesting.com
Printed in the USA
LVOW06s1554251115

464204LV00008B/801/P